Healthy Honey COOKBOOK

Second Edition

Larry Lonik

D1226159

STACKPOLE BOOKS

0 11557 01195 1

Published by
STACKPOLE BOOKS
5067 Ritter Road
Mechanicsburg, PA 17055
www.stackpolebooks.com

Printed in the United States

10 9 8 7 6 5 4 3 2 1

Cover design by Tessa Sweigert
Cover photo courtesy of the Agricultural Research Service, USDA, Scott Bauer, photographer
Recipes in the beauty chapter and updated information about honey courtesy of the National Honey Board, www.honey.com
Information about honeybees from Texas A&M University Honey Bee Information, http://honeybee.tamu.edu, and the American Beekeeping Federation, www.abfnet.org

Library of Congress Cataloging-in-Publication Data
Lonik, Larry James.
  [Healthy taste of honey.]
  Healthy honey cookbook : recipes, anecdotes, and lore / Larry Lonik. -- Second edition.
      pages cm
  Includes index.
  Revision of the author's Healthy taste of honey. Virginia Beach : Donning, 1981.
  ISBN-13: 978-0-8117-1195-1 (pbk.)
  ISBN-10: 0-8117-1195-1 (pbk.)
  1. Cooking (Honey) I. Title.
  TX767.H7L68 2013
  641.6'8—dc23
                                                    2012039870

Contents

Honeybees

Honeybees are the most pleasant, sociable, genial, and good-natured little beings that can be encountered in all animated creation—when they are understood.

Honeybees have hairy bodies compared to wasps' smooth ones. Pollen is the only source of protein for honeybees, whose hairy bodies aid in collecting pollen. Another major difference is that a honeybee is able to sting only one time and dies soon after. The honeybee stinger has small hooks that cause the stinger to remain embedded in the victim. The sting apparatus is pulled from the bee's body when the bee moves away, causing massive abdominal rupture and death. A wasp has a smooth stinger and may sting many times.

Bumblebees also gather pollen as a source of protein and have hairy bodies, but bumblebees' bodies are more square-shaped and have more hair than the honeybee's body. Bumblebees can sting many times, like wasps. Sometimes a fly is confused with a bee, but flies have only one pair of wings. Honeybees and other bees, ants, and wasps belonging to the order Hymenoptera have two pairs of clear wings.

There are three kinds of members of a honeybee colony:

Queen: mother to all the bees in the colony; she is a fertile female.

Worker: an infertile female that performs the labor tasks of the colony, including feed preparation; guarding the hive; feeding the queens, drones, and brood; and heating and cooling the hive.

Drone: the male that starts out as an unfertilized egg. Its only purpose in the colony is to mate with a virgin queen. They live to mate with the queen, but not more than one in a thousand get the opportunity to mate.

About one-third of the total human diet is derived directly or indirectly from insect-pollinated plants. An estimated 80 percent of insect crop pollination is accomplished by honeybees. Honeybees are needed to pollinate a variety of fruits, berries, vegetables, tree nuts, oil seeds, and legumes. Of the 100 crop species that provide 90 percent of the world's food, more than 70 are pollinated by bees, according to a 2011 U.N. environmental agency report.

STINGING

The average beekeeper may get stung 20 times in his daily routine, but he knows the habits of his bees and realizes that a sting causes him very little harm. On the other hand, there is a general impression that bees are always in a towering rage, ready to inflict pain on everything and everybody coming near them. Is the fear of pain greater than the pain itself? Is there reason for a human being 260,000 times the size of a honeybee to avoid this tiny creature? Perhaps a glimpse at some of the habits of this insect and the conditions that affect its disposition can lead us to a better understanding of the honeybee and its sting as well as ways to avoid (or live with) it.

The honeybee is the most common species of stinging insect in the United States. Bees and the related wasps, hornets, yellow jackets, and ants generally will sting for one of two reasons: because they need to protect their home or because something has gone wrong. Bees are temperamental and, like humans, have their good and bad days. External forces affect their disposition. Because bees are usually not active at temperatures below 55 degrees Fahrenheit or on rainy days, the bees remain around or in the hive—making cold, wet days definitely a bad time for hive inspection. Things that may go wrong and make bees cross include scarcity of food or water, bad weather conditions, or poor honey flow in the hive. When a beekeeper removes honey from the hive, he should take care to leave adequate stores for the bees.

As food supplies diminish, usually in the month of August, incidents of reported stings are at their highest. Bees are attracted to sweets and their fragrances, which are the basic attraction that flowering plants have for them. Recently shampooed hair, powders, deodorants, colognes, or perfumes often will influence a scouting bee to investigate the source. The approach of a bee in this situation is usually cautious and unthreatening. Most often, the bee will realize the subject of its investigation is not a viable food source and will pass. If you swat at it, the bee may believe it and its colony are being attacked; counterattack may be the reaction. Many stings could be avoided by not swatting at an investigative honeybee. I have found it fascinating to watch these creatures in their harmless pursuits. A word of caution, however: avoid bees getting near the face and hair. If a bee happens to get into the hair, or near it, the bee may consider the strands as some kind of trap and counterattack may, again, be the reaction. A slow, steady movement of the hand and arm can usually keep a bee at a safe distance and away from a mutually undesirable situation.

A colony of honeybees sends out scouts to find sources of nectar and pollen. Only after the scouts return and the colony democratically "votes" on which supply they will gather does the mass of bees begin foraging. Food, beer, or soda pop may cause scouting bees (usually singly or in a small group) to check out a possible food source. Because the bees are looking for steady, abundant supplies, a can of pop or even a relatively large picnic spread is usually determined by the scouts to be temporary, small, and undesirable.

The important point to remember here is that honeybees do not want to sting—especially something the size of a human being. A stinger embedded in flesh will almost always result in the death of the bee. The stinger has recurved barbs that are held in flesh, and the stinger and venom sac are torn from the bee, ultimately killing the worker. (Drones, the males, have no stingers.)

What happens if a sting does occur? It is important to remove the stinger the moment it is given. Quickly rub or scratch the stinger out with a knife blade or fingernail, being careful not to break it off in the skin. Do not squeeze or pinch because that action might push more poison into the wound. In most cases, bee stings cause only a local reaction with pain lasting for several minutes. A redness and slight swelling may occur. Apply a cold compress. Seek medical help immediately if breathing is difficult, you have been stung many times, or you are allergic to bee stings.

About 2 percent of the human populace has some kind of hypersensitive reaction to bee stings. Symptoms in an allergic person usually appear within a few minutes, but may not show up for 24 hours. In these cases, local swelling may be excessive or a hivelike condition may break out over the body. Difficulty in breathing may follow, with the lips turning blue. Vomiting and loss of consciousness may follow also. A physician should be called immediately. Medical treatments are effective, and eventual desensitization is possible in most cases. Emergency kits are available for people with severe reactions. For the vast nonallergic majority, however, pain from a sting quickly disappears. A hot compress is a simple, quick remedy to ease any pain.

Honeybees are basically harmless, manageable creatures. Evidence from early Roman and Greek writers shows that attempts to manipulate bees were made long ago and that experiments have been noted ever since.

The most celebrated beekeeper is the eighteenth-century Englishman Daniel Wildman. Known as "Wildman the Bee Man," he traveled throughout Europe exhibiting his bee-taming talents. He reportedly could command his bees to settle on any designated part of his body, and he once was carried through the streets of London in a chair completely covered with bees. He also did battle against mad dogs, armed only with a swarm of bees.

Today state and county fairs across the United States often have exhibits in which a beekeeper dons a "bee beard" or "bee gloves" or performs some other feat with live bees. The purpose of these demonstrations is to show the safety with which a trained, knowledgeable person can handle bees. Only people who have specialized training, however, should attempt any experiment mentioned here.

Gaining knowledge about the honeybee and understanding and using that knowledge are the keys to our peaceful, safe, and beneficial coexistence with these creative, industrious creatures.

LEGENDS AND LORE

It seems hardly possible to imagine a time when honeybees were not plentiful in North America, but, even though the bee has a much longer history than humanity, the honeybee is not a native American. It was introduced to this continent by early settlers. The first beekeepers in the United States were mysterious figures, included by many authors as one of the legendary characters of the Old West. Along with the blacksmith, the scout, and the trapper, the beekeeper invariably appears in novels by James Fenimore Cooper, Zane Grey, and others. Beekeepers were always intriguing and "magical" personages, respected as well as feared. The mystique of these early characters was rooted in legend and lore that had developed in Europe. To understand beekeeping in the young United States and its development to its present state, we must look at bees and beekeepers before they crossed the Atlantic.

Since earliest recorded history, the moralist, the philosopher, the artist, the engineer, the poet, and the political scientist all have contemplated the honeybee with a sense of humility and awe. This tiny creature has been the object of study and experimentation from the cradles of civilization onward. Monuments in Egypt dating from as early as 3500 B.C. depict bees. (The price of honey at that time was about five cents a quart.) Hieroglyphic symbols show that the bee was chosen to represent a king, linking bees with both the gods and mortal royalty. In Indian philosophy, Vishnu—one of the great triad of Brahma, Vishnu, and Siva—was represented as a blue bee resting on a lotus blossom. Fascination and reverence for the honeybee color the tales and legends in these ancient civilizations.

An ancient Greek myth relates that sacred bees nourished and protected the infant Zeus when he was hidden in a cave in Crete. Honey, it was said, was the sole food of the child, the future chief of the gods of Mount Olympus. In consequence, he was sometimes called the Bee Man. It is from the ancient Greeks that many superstitions, stories, and ideas about honey began in Europe. Honey, gathered in conjunction with the rising of Venus, Jupiter, or Mercury, was believed to have the power to cure diseases of the eyes, bowels, and ulcers and actually to restore life to the dead.

Religious practices and values aided the spread of beekeeping. Beeswax used for ceremonial candles gave the apiarist another market for his profession. The bee was adopted by many religious groups because, in addition to the value of the insect as a provider of honey and wax, its virtues of chastity, frugality, and industry were extolled by church leaders. The Book of Mormon, first printed in 1830, signifies the place of the bee in religious literature, as does the Koran chapter entitled "The Bee." According to Mohammed, this insect is the only creature ever directly spoken to by the Lord.

Napoleon Bonaparte's fascination with the industry and efficiency of bees led him to decorate his coat of arms and clothing with embroidered bees.

European bee lore was carried eastward across the Atlantic Ocean to North America. Bees were respected as moralists, stinging those given to profanity as a reminder of their sins. Whittier's poem "Telling the Bees" relates the curious ritual of talking to the bees in the hive, informing the colony of events in the life of their beekeeper. This custom arose from the European traditions that bees were unable to prosper after the death of their master and that if swarms were not cared for, the owner would die. If the family of the beekeeper were to celebrate without paying due respect to the hive—often decorating the structure itself with scarlet ribbon or cloth—the bees would leave.

It has been said that one cannot get stung while working in the beeyard if one holds one's breath. Stolen swarms supposedly cannot survive. Burying the liver of a white falcon or the eye of a bear beneath the hive is an infallible method of ensuring the bees within. These and other beliefs and superstitions about how to control swarms, how to make bees thrive, and how to avoid stings traveled across the ocean with the first transatlantic honeybees.

The actual date of importation of the first colonies of honeybees is unknown, though it was in the early colonial days. Beekeeping records from 1622 have been found in Virginia. In 1763, the English introduced colonies of bees in Florida. In 1773, a single colony was taken from Florida to Mobile, Alabama. By 1800, honeybees were fairly common throughout the eastern half of the continent.

Beekeeping in the American colonies around 1670 declined because of the disease known as American foulbrood. Care and inspection methods were primitive at the time, and the situation did not change for 150 years. Moses Quimby of New York and the Reverend Lorenzo Langstroth of Andover, Massachusetts, revolutionized the bee industry, and the golden age of beekeeping began. From around 1830 to the beginning of World War I, virtually all of the equipment and beekeeping methods used today were devised. Langstroth introduced the movable-frame hive and the theory of "bee space" that ensured the success of the hive.

The Industrial Revolution greatly affected the beekeeping industry in the United States. Machine production of standard-sized interchangeable frames and hives, the wax comb foundation, and the centrifugal honey extractor completed the evolution of beekeeping to its present commercial status. Further developments have been processes of refinement rather than innovation.

The honeybees in North America, until 1850, were descendants of British and German stocks brought here by the early colonists. They were difficult to handle and susceptible to disease. After many disappointments, three significantly superior races were established in the United States: the Italian, the Caucasian, and the Carniolan races. In this golden age of beekeeping, the new stocks spread rapidly across the country, aided by the development of a way to ship queens through the mail and by new methods of queen rearing.

Today, apicultural research facilities have been established. In addition to its importance as a producer of honey and wax and as a pollinator, the honeybee is now a research animal in biological and medicinal studies. Advances in controlled mating and artificial insemination will further enhance production and control in the future. Interestingly, as the industry has become increasingly commercialized, beekeeping as a hobby has been on the increase. The modern era has let the air out of many old superstitions and beliefs, but human fascination with the honeybee is still there and rightly so.

BEES TODAY

Stories about killer bees materialized after 26 swarms led by queens from Africa escaped in Brazil in 1957. The hybrid Africanized bees have spread over the Americas. African bees produce swarms up to 12 times a year, compared with once a year for bees common to the United States. They are more easily provoked than European honeybees and can travel great distances. When disturbed they defend themselves with persistence and ferocity not found among European types. Their sting, though, is no more potent than that of other honeybees.

The honeybee is a social creature, relying on the colony to exist. The colony, in turn, relies on the individual bee to do its assigned tasks.

Beginning in early 2007, beekeepers have seen a marked decline in bee populations in the United States and around the world. The U.S. Department of Agriculture reported that U.S. honey-producing colonies dropped from a population of 5.5 million in 1950 to 2.5 million in 2007. Two recent studies have linked this decline, now called colony collapse disorder (CCD), to the use of a newer type of pesticide called neonicotinoids, which emerged in the mid-1990s as a safer alternative to more damaging pesticides. Other causes have been proposed, such as mites, parasites, and insect diseases and other environmental changes. A 2010 study suggests a combination of factors may cause the disorder.

Beverages

HONEYED FRUIT PUNCH

Yield: 6 servings

1 cup orange juice
$\frac{1}{2}$ cup lemon juice
2 cups grape juice
2 cups water
4 tablespoons honey

Mix thoroughly. Chill. Serve cold.

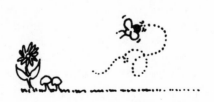

HOT MULLED CIDER

Yield: 6 servings

1 quart apple cider
$1/2$ cup honey
6 lemon slices
12 whole cloves
$1/8$ teaspoon ground nutmeg
6 cinnamon sticks

In a saucepan, combine all ingredients except cinnamon sticks. Simmer 8–10 minutes. Pour into six mugs, removing lemon slices if desired. Add a cinnamon stick to each mug for stirring.

HONEY HOT CHOCOLATE

Yield: 2–3 servings

$1\frac{1}{4}$ cups water
pinch of salt
1 tablespoon unsweetened cocoa
1 tablespoon honey
$3/4$ cup milk

In a saucepan, stir together water, salt, and cocoa. Simmer 2 minutes until smooth. Add honey and milk; stir and heat without boiling.

> *The stinger of a honeybee has recurved (slanted away from the direction of entry) barbs. If the stinger enters another insect, the stinger will deposit its venom and be retracted without harm to the bee. If the stinger is inserted into the flesh of an animal, however, it cannot be pulled out because of the barbs. The bee will die as its body and the stinger separate. The stinger continues to bore deeper into the flesh, by reflex movements, and to release poison into the wound.*

INSTANT BREAKFAST DRINK

Yield: 1 serving

  ½ cup orange juice
  ½ cup milk
  1 teaspoon lemon juice
  2 tablespoons honey
  1 egg
  dash of ground nutmeg

Combine ingredients and beat vigorously until foamy or whirl in a blender until frothy. Pour into a tall glass. This delicious instant breakfast contains all the essentials of a balanced day-starter.

> *My son, eat thou honey, because it is good; and the honeycomb, which is sweet to the taste.*
>
> *—Proverbs 24:13*

HONEY-BERRY LEMONADE

Yield: 4–5 servings

  4 large lemons
  ½ cup honey
  3½ cups water
  1 cup berries (blueberries, strawberries, raspberries)

Squeeze lemons and strain juice. Add most of the honey and mix well. Add to water. Add berries. Use the remaining honey to sweeten to taste. Partially fill frosted glasses with ice cubes, pour in lemonade, and garnish with a sprig of mint.

> *The true honeybee was not known in the Americas until Spanish, Dutch, and English settlers introduced it near the end of the seventeenth century.*

HONEY MILK PUNCH

Yield: 4 servings

6 eggs, beaten until fluffy
³/₄ cup honey
1 whole nutmeg or ¹/₂ teaspoon ground nutmeg
1 quart whole milk

Beat honey gradually into eggs; set aside. Add nutmeg to milk. Heat, without boiling, until beads form around the edge of the pan. Add milk to egg and honey mixture slowly, stirring constantly. Pour into cups and sprinkle a little nutmeg on top.

HONEY EGGNOG PUNCH

Yield: 6–8 servings

6 eggs
2 tablespoons honey
1 pint whiskey
1 pint milk
3 ounces light rum
1 pint whipping cream, lightly whipped
nutmeg

Separate eggs. Beat yolks and honey until light. Add whiskey, milk, rum, and lightly whipped cream. Beat egg whites until stiff and add to the mixture. Chill at least 3 hours. Serve with a dusting of nutmeg.

> *One of the most popular characters from the television series* **Romper Room** *was the* **Do Bee,** *who taught the Golden Rule, etiquette, justice, morality, reason, right from wrong, and good from bad.*

> *Americans consume an average of*
> *285 million pounds of honey every year.*

HONEYSUCKLE

Yield: 1 serving

> 1 teaspoon honey
> ¹/₂ cup lemon juice
> 1¹/₂–2 ounces rum

Mix honey and lemon juice together. Add rum. Pour onto cracked ice. Strain into a well-chilled cocktail glass.

HONEY ZOMBIE

Yield: 1 tall serving

> 1 teaspoon clover honey
> juice of 1 lime
> 1¹/₂ ounces heavy rum
> 2 ounces dark rum
> 2 ounces light rum
> 1¹/₂ ounces pineapple juice
> 1¹/₂ ounces papaya juice
> dash of apricot brandy
> pineapple stick
> maraschino cherry

Mix together all ingredients except for the pineapple stick and cherry. Pour into a highball glass. Garnish with pineapple and cherry.

HONEY SLUSH

Yield: 20 servings

1 can (12 ounces) frozen cranberry juice
1 can (12 ounces) frozen orange juice
1 can (12 ounces) frozen lemonade
8 cups water
2 cups honey
2 cups liquor (not rum)
7-Up

Thaw frozen juices and mix thoroughly with water, honey, and liquor. Freeze in a 5-quart container. To serve, scoop mixture into glasses and add 7-Up.

BEES KNEES

Yield: 1 serving

1¼ ounces gin
1 tablespoon honey
¾ ounce lemon juice
lemon shavings

Blend until frothy. Serve on ice.

Bees are masters of efficiency. Three thousand bees can fly for an hour on a single ounce of sugar (fuel). When flying, a bee beats its wings up and down 200 times per second.

HONEY BLOSSOM

Yield: 1 serving

1¹/₂–2 ounces gin
¹/₂ ounce orange juice
¹/₂ teaspoon honey
dash of lime juice
orange slice

Mix all ingredients well with cracked ice. Strain into a well-chilled cocktail glass. Garnish with an orange slice.

HONEY COCKTAIL

Yield: 12–14 servings

1 cup honey
1 cup warm water
1 cup rum
1 cup brandy
1¹/₂ cups milk
1¹/₂ cups whipping cream
12 eggs
ginger

Combine and beat honey, water, rum, and brandy. Slowly add milk, cream, and eggs, whipping until foamy. Serve in glasses with a light dusting of ginger.

> *Most bee and insect colonies are annual,*
> *with all but the queen dying in the fall.*
> *Not so with the honeybee, who must provide*
> *for the future in its perennial existence.*

HONEY SOUR

Yield: 1 serving

1½ ounces lemon juice
½ teaspoon honey
1½ ounces blended whiskey (or Scotch or rum)
maraschino cherry

Mix juice, honey, and whiskey together with cracked ice. Strain into a sour glass. Add cherry.

> *Honeybees learn to recognize the species of flower*
> *they are exploiting on the basis of its color,*
> *outline, odor, location, nearby landmarks,*
> *and time of nectar production.*

CARROT-TOP TEA

Yield: 4 servings

4 cups hot water
6 carrot tops, medium-sized
1 small piece orange peel
honey

Pour hot water over carrot tops and orange peel. Let steep. Sweeten with honey to taste.

ORANGE-LEMON PUNCH FOR A CROWD

Yield: 16 servings

2 cups boiling water
8 teaspoons tea leaves
1½ cups honey
1 cup lemon juice
5 cups orange juice
2 quarts iced water or iced tea

Pour boiling water over tea and steep 5 minutes. Strain. Dissolve honey in the warm tea. Let cool, and then combine with remaining ingredients.

Suggestions: Use less liquid in the punch and serve over a block of ice in a punch bowl; garnish with orange and lemon slices. Premix honey, tea, and juices to refill the bowl as needed. Experiment with flavored teas.

HONEY PARTY PUNCH

Yield: 40 servings

2 cups honey
1 cup hot water
1 cup lemon juice
3 cups orange juice
3 quarts unsweetened pineapple juice
1 cup mint leaves (optional)
3 quarts water
4 quarts ginger ale
1 cup maraschino cherries

Add honey to hot water. Add fruit juices, mint, and 3 quarts of water. Chill. Just before serving, add ginger ale and cherries. Pour over ice.

HONEY LEMON CLARET

Yield: 1 serving

$1/2$ teaspoon honey
juice of 1 lemon
3 ounces claret
soda

Mix honey and lemon juice in a highball glass. Add ice and claret. Add soda and stir. Variations: Experiment with different wines.

The largest beehive on record was discovered at the top of a 150-foot eucalyptus tree in Australia in 1979. The hive measured 36 feet in height and 21 feet in diameter. It weighed 10 tons and yielded 7,000 pounds of honey.

HOT HONEY WINE

Yield: 1 serving

1 egg yolk
2 ounces honey
6 ounces red wine
$1/2$ ounce Curaçao
lemon slice

Combine egg yolk and honey in a saucepan; blend well. Add wine and Curaçao. Heat till almost boiling. Serve in a hot mug with a lemon slice; sprinkle with ground cinnamon.

> *Honey was used to make mead, an early ale that*
> *supposedly made men strong and brawny.*

WOLVERINE MEAD

Yield: 4–5 quarts

4–4¹/₂ pounds honey
2¹/₂ quarts water
¹/₄ ounce citric acid
5 ounces strong, freshly made tea
1 package wine yeast
2 teaspoons yeast nutrient

Mix honey with water. Bring to a boil and boil 2 minutes. Pour into a clean plastic pail. Add citric acid and tea. Add more hot water until mixture totals 5 quarts. Mix. Cool to 65 degrees. Add yeast and nutrient. Cover pail with a plastic sheet; seal around the top with string or a rubber band. Ferment in a warm place 10–14 days. Pour into jars, leaving behind as much sediment as possible. Put a fermentation lock on the jars and leave for 2 months. When liquid is clear, bottle it and age 9–12 months before serving.

LONIKA LUA HOMEMADE KAHLUA

Yield: 2 quarts

3 cups honey
4 cups water
16 teaspoons instant coffee powder
1¹/₂ cups vodka
3 teaspoons vanilla

Simmer honey, water, and coffee for 2 hours, stirring occasionally. Temperature should be so low that the surface barely moves; be careful not to burn or heat too fast. Let cool to room temperature. Add vodka and vanilla. Bottle what you can't drink.

BLACK RUSSIAN

Yield: 1 serving

1½ ounces Lonika Lua Homemade Kahlua
1½ ounces vodka

Combine and serve over crushed ice.

WHITE RUSSIAN

Yield: 1 serving

1½ ounces Lonika Lua Homemade Kahlua
1½ ounces vodka
1½ ounces cream

Combine and serve over crushed ice.

> *To him who has known them and loved them,*
> *a summer where there are no bees becomes as sad*
> *and as empty as one without flowers or birds.*
>
> —*Maurice Maeterlinck,* **The Life of the Bee**

Salads and Salad Dressings

HARVEST MOON SALAD

Yield: 6 servings

1 clove garlic
1 head lettuce
3 tablespoons honey
2 cups cooked ham and turkey strips
$\frac{1}{2}$ pound sharp cheddar cheese
4 hard-cooked eggs, sliced in rounds
1 green pepper, cut in strips
1 bunch radishes, sliced
$\frac{1}{2}$ teaspoon salt
freshly ground pepper

Rub a salad bowl with peeled clove of garlic. Separate lettuce leaves and line salad bowl with leaves. Lightly dribble honey over lettuce. Arrange on top of lettuce the following: ham, turkey, and cheese strips; hard-cooked eggs; green pepper strips; sliced radishes. Sprinkle with salt and pepper. Serve with Perk-Up Salad Dressing (see page 32).

COLESLAW

Yield: 4–5 servings

1 cup sour cream
¼ cup honey
1 teaspoon salt
2 teaspoons celery salt
4 cups shredded cabbage

Combine first four ingredients and pour over cabbage.

Honeybee, Latin: **Apis mellifera** *Linnaeus*

PONDEROSA COLESLAW

Yield: 10–12 servings

1 cup honey
1 cup cider or wine vinegar
½ cup finely chopped onion
1 teaspoon salt
1 teaspoon celery seed (optional)
1 large head cabbage, finely chopped, about 4 cups
1 cup diced green pepper
1 cup diced celery

In a small saucepan, combine honey with vinegar, onion, salt, and celery seed. Bring to a boil; reduce heat and simmer 5 minutes. Cool. Pour the cooled dressing over prepared vegetables and toss lightly. Cover and chill overnight to blend flavors.

CARROT RAISIN SALAD

Yield: 8 half-cup servings

> 3 cups raw shredded carrots
> 1 cup seedless raisins
> 1/3 cup mayonnaise or salad dressing
> 1/4 cup milk
> 1 tablespoon honey
> 1 tablespoon lemon juice
> 1/4 teaspoon salt

Toss carrots together with raisins. Blend remaining ingredients together to make dressing and mix into carrot/raisin mixture. Refrigerate for about 30 minutes.

A social and charitable custom among many peoples for many years is often known as a "sewing bee" or "quilting bee." Still today there are groups who meet and donate their time and energy to make a product that may provide needed funds for a particular charity.

COOKOUT BEAN SALAD

Yield: 12 servings

1 can (16 ounces) cut wax beans
1 can (16 ounces) cut green beans
1 can (16 ounces) green lima beans
1 can (16 ounces) red kidney beans
1 green pepper, thinly sliced
1 medium red onion, thinly sliced in rings
$\frac{1}{2}$ cup honey
$\frac{1}{2}$ cup vinegar
1 teaspoon seasoned salt
$\frac{1}{2}$ teaspoon dry mustard
1 tablespoon chopped chives

Drain all beans thoroughly. Combine beans with peppers and onions. Blend together remaining ingredients and pour over vegetables. Cover and marinate in refrigerator overnight, stirring once or twice. Drain and serve.

APPLE-PEANUT SALAD

Yield: 6 servings

3 cups diced unpeeled red apples
1 cup diced celery
$\frac{3}{4}$ cup salted peanuts
$\frac{1}{2}$ cup mayonnaise
3 tablespoons honey
1 teaspoon celery seed
salad greens (optional)

Place apples, celery, and peanuts into a bowl. Mix remaining ingredients, except for greens, and pour over mixture in bowl. Stir to coat and serve on greens, if desired.

> *Honey is a remedy for all diseases.*
>
> *—Mohammed*

TANGY WALDORF SALAD

Yield: 6 servings

>3 cups diced unpeeled red apples (2 to 3 medium-sized)
>1 cup sliced celery
>$^1/_2$ cup sweet pickle relish, drained
>$^1/_2$ cup coarsely chopped walnuts
>3 tablespoons honey
>3 tablespoons sour cream or mayonnaise
>$^1/_4$ teaspoon salt
>6 crisp lettuce cups

Lightly toss apples, celery, relish, and nuts together. Blend honey with sour cream or mayonnaise and salt. Pour over apple mixture and lightly toss. Chill. Serve in lettuce cups.

FROZEN STRAWBERRY SALAD

Yield: 4–5 servings

>1 envelope unflavored gelatin
>$^1/_4$ cup water
>1 can (13$^1/_4$ ounces) pineapple tidbits, undrained
>1 tablespoon lemon juice
>$^1/_8$ teaspoon salt
>$^1/_8$ teaspoon ground ginger
>2 tablespoons honey
>1 pint strawberries, sliced
>$^1/_2$ cup heavy cream, whipped
>$^1/_2$ cup mayonnaise
>salad greens
>whole strawberries
>watercress (optional)

In the top of a double boiler, dissolve gelatin in ¼ cup water. Add pineapple and syrup, lemon juice, salt, ginger, and honey. Mix well. Add sliced strawberries and chill until slightly thickened. Mix cream and mayonnaise and fold into fruit mixture. Pour into a 9-by-5-by-3-inch loaf pan (pan will be about half full). Freeze until firm. Turn onto a cutting board or platter and cut 8 to 10 slices. For each serving, arrange 2 slices on greens. Garnish with whole strawberries and watercress, if desired. If salad is frozen solid, let stand at room temperature for about 30 minutes before serving.

The opening game of the 1977 baseball season, televised nationally from Los Angeles, was delayed for an hour because a swarm of bees had settled in a player dugout. A beekeeper had to be called in to remove the bees.

HONEY FRUIT MELANGE

Yield: 4–6 servings

4 cups assorted fruit, cut up
½ cup honey
1 tablespoon fresh chopped candied ginger
1 tablespoon lemon juice

Place fruit in a serving bowl or refrigerator dish. Combine honey, candied ginger, and lemon juice; pour mixture over fruit and chill for 2 hours. In the winter, use grapefruit and orange sections, fresh pineapple, bananas, and red grapes. In the summer, combine a mixture of melons, berries, peaches, and pears.

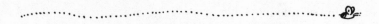

Annual honey production worldwide is 600,000 tons.

PINK SHRIMP-ORANGE SALAD

Yield: 6 servings

3 medium-sized oranges, peeled and cut in bite-sized pieces
(about 1¹/₂ cups)
¹/₂ cup celery
¹/₂ cup sliced ripe olives
¹/₂ pound cleaned, cooked shrimp
2 tablespoons chopped onion
¹/₄ teaspoon salt
¹/₂ cup honey dressing of your choice (see California Fruit
Salad Dressing, page 32, or Honey Fruit Dressing,
page 34)
6 crisp lettuce cups

Combine orange pieces, celery, olives, shrimp, chopped onion, and
salt; blend with dressing to moisten. Chill. Serve in lettuce cups on
individual salad plates, topped with more honey dressing.

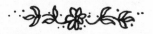

*A bee larva is originally nursed on rich royal jelly
for the first 60 hours and then honey and pollen
for the next 84 hours. In this six-day period a larva
gains 1,500 times its weight. It sheds its skin
once a day for the first four days.*

SPRINGTIME SALAD

Yield: 6 servings

3 large oranges, peeled
2 large, firm, ripe bananas
Honey Fruit Dressing (page 34)
salad greens
1/3 cup chopped walnuts

Slice peeled oranges into cartwheels. Peel bananas; slice in half lengthwise, then into 2-inch pieces. Pour Honey Fruit Dressing over fruit pieces and chill 30 minutes. Drain fruit and arrange attractively over crisp salad greens. Sprinkle with walnuts and serve with remaining dressing.

HONEY SOY DRESSING

Yield: 2 cups

1/2 cup lemon juice
1/3 cup honey
1/2 teaspoon grated lemon peel
1 drop mint extract
1/2 cup vegetable oil
2 tablespoons toasted sesame seeds
1 teaspoon soy sauce
dash of salt

Toast sesame seeds in a 350-degree oven until light golden brown. Shake ingredients together in a covered jar. Chill.

POPPY SEED SALAD DRESSING

Yield: 2 cups

$1/3$ cup honey
$1/2$ teaspoon salt
$1/3$ cup vinegar
3 tablespoons dry mustard
$1^1/4$ cups vegetable oil
$2^1/2$ tablespoons poppy seeds

Mix ingredients together in the above order. Blend with an electric mixer or in a blender until the oil is well incorporated.

> *Honeybees, like all insects, can distinguish four qualities of taste: sweet, bitter, salty, and sour.*

HONEY SALAD DRESSING

Yield: 4–8 cups

2–3 cups sugar
1 teaspoon dry mustard
1 teaspoon ground paprika
$1/4$ teaspoon salt
1 teaspoon celery seed
1–3 cups honey
1–3 cups vinegar
1 tablespoon lemon juice
1 teaspoon grated onion
1 cup vegetable oil

Combine ingredients and beat with a rotary beater until blended. Use on any canned or fresh fruit or tossed green lettuce salad.

SWEET-SOUR SALAD DRESSING

Yield: 2 cups

 4 slices bacon
 2 tablespoons finely chopped onion
 ¼ cup honey
 ¼ cup vinegar
 ½ cup water
 1 cup bottled Italian-style salad dressing

Fry bacon until crisp; remove and drain on paper towel. Crumble into small pieces and set aside. Sauté onion in bacon drippings until tender. Pour off all but 1 tablespoon of bacon drippings. Add honey, vinegar, and water. Bring to a boil. Cool. Combine cooled mixture with bottled salad dressing and beat or blend. Stir in bacon pieces. Chill. Shake well before using.

FRENCH HONEY DRESSING

Yield: 2 cups

 ½ cup vegetable oil
 ½ cup honey
 1¼ cups ketchup
 1 teaspoon salt
 2 tablespoons lemon juice
 finely grated onion, to taste

Beat all ingredients well or combine in a blender. Store in refrigerator.

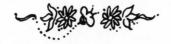

In a cave in Spain, a painting at least 7,000 years old shows honey being collected from a bee's nest.

PERK-UP SALAD DRESSING

Yield: 1¹/₂ cups

1 can (10¹/₂ ounces) condensed tomato soup, undiluted
1 clove garlic, minced
2 tablespoons honey
¹/₂ teaspoon salt
¹/₄ teaspoon crushed dill or tarragon
¹/₃ cup lemon juice or white wine vinegar

In a blender, combine all ingredients. Cover and blend 5 seconds.
Chill before serving over assorted salad greens.

> *When bees "swarm," about half the membership and*
> *the present queen will leave to find a new colony. They*
> *leave several capped queen cells behind, one of which*
> *will hatch into a new queen for the parent colony.*

CALIFORNIA FRUIT SALAD DRESSING

Make a colorful arrangement of fresh fruits on a serving platter. For
dressing, sweeten 1 cup of sour cream with 1 or 2 tablespoons of
honey.

> *Honey is able to absorb moisture*
> *from anything—even metal and stone.*

HONEY CREAM DRESSING

Yield: 1¹/₂ cups

1 cup sour cream
2 tablespoons honey
2 tablespoons grapefruit juice
2 tablespoons orange juice

Blend and refrigerate.

ORANGE FRUIT DRESSING

Yield: 1¹/₂ cups

1 cup mayonnaise
¹/₄ cup honey
1 tablespoon grated orange peel
1 tablespoon orange juice

Combine and chill. Serve over drained chilled fruit.

Honeybees will go miles for pollen and nectar, but they will usually pollinate flowers more thoroughly within 100 yards of their colonies.

Honeybees are born in the hive, and while they develop, they learn the tasks of the hive, progressing to more important tasks as they grow older. They finally qualify as scouts and foragers, leaving the hive to find and collect nectar and pollen. They fly until they literally shred their wings in their efforts for their queen—and then die. The entire lifespan of the female honeybee is approximately six weeks during the peak pollen season.

HONEY FRUIT DRESSING

Blend 1 part yogurt with 1 part honey. Serve with any fruit combination.

For catalysts in our nutrition we turn to the trace minerals found in fruits, berries, edible leaves, edible roots, and honey. One or two teaspoons of honey taken at every meal will provide the catalysts needed to speed up the handling of food by the body.

HONEY LIME DRESSING

Yield: 1¹/₂ cups

> 1 can (6 ounces) frozen limeade concentrate
> ³/₄ cup vegetable oil
> ¹/₂ cup honey
> ¹/₄ teaspoon salt
> 2 teaspoons celery seed

Place limeade, oil, honey, and salt in a blender container; blend a few seconds. Stir in celery seed. Beat or shake to mix. Serve over fruit salad.

About 21 days after the bee egg is laid, the newly born worker will emerge. The queen will hatch in about 16 days, drones in about 25 days.

MINT FRUIT SALAD DRESSING

Yield: 1¹/₂ cups

   ¹/₂ cup honey
   ¹/₂ cup water
   ¹/₂ teaspoon ground cardamom (optional)
   1 teaspoon crushed mint leaves
   1 teaspoon grated lemon juice
   ¹/₈ teaspoon salt
   ¹/₄ cup vegetable oil

Combine honey, water, and cardamom in a small saucepan. Bring to a boil and simmer about 3 minutes. Remove from heat and add mint. Chill until cool. Strain. Add remaining ingredients and shake or mix well to blend. Chill.

··✺✾✾✺·❀✺✾··

Beeswax is secreted from the glands
of the bee's lower abdomen.

Pickles and Preserves

FRUIT PRESERVE SYRUP

Yield: 2–4 cups

2 cups honey
3¹/₂ cups water
¹/₄–¹/₂ teaspoon ascorbic acid

Make a syrup by bringing to a boil the honey and water. Before using syrup, mix in ¹/₄ teaspoon ascorbic acid per 2 cups of syrup.

For canning: use warm syrup.

For freezing: chill syrup and use to prevent discoloration of apples, peaches, apricots, and pears.

> *Madam, treat your husband with honey*
> *and you will possess his heart.*
>
> **—Old Roman Saying**

SWEET FRUIT PICKLES

Yield: 5–6 pints

2 cups honey
1 cup vinegar
2 inches stick cinnamon
6 whole cloves
4 pounds whole crabapples

Combine honey, vinegar, and spices; heat to boiling. Cook 2 or 3 cups of apples at a time in the syrup, handling gently so they will not mash. When transparent, lift out and place in a jar or bowl and continue until all are cooked. Take out spices, pour remaining syrup over apples, and seal in sterilized jars. Serve chilled, with meats.

HONEY MELON PICKLES

Yield: four 1/2-pint jars

8 cups watermelon rind

SYRUP
4 cups water
1 cup pickling salt
1 cup vinegar
1/4 cup water
3 1/2 cups honey
1/8 teaspoon oil of cloves
1/4 teaspoon oil of cinnamon
few drops of red or green food coloring

To prepare watermelon rind, remove the rind from a watermelon, separating all red fruit from the rind. Cut rind in 1-by-3-inch strips. Cover 8 cups of rind strips with salted water and soak overnight. Rinse and drain. Cook rind in fresh water until fork-tender; drain.

Prepare syrup. Combine ingredients, coloring as desired. Cook syrup until dissolved. Add drained watermelon rind and simmer 8–10 minutes. Pack in sterile jars and seal. Age 3–4 weeks before using.

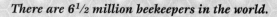

There are 6½ million beekeepers in the world.

BREAD AND BUTTER PICKLES

Yield: 4 quarts

1 cup salt
2 quarts water
4 quarts sliced cucumbers
5 cups honey
3 cups vinegar
1 tablespoon celery seed
1 tablespoon mustard seed

Prepare a brine by combining salt and water. Soak cucumbers in brine for 1 hour. Prepare a syrup by combining honey, vinegar, celery seed, and mustard seed. Bring to a full boil, and then simmer for 5 minutes. Drop drained cucumbers into syrup and cook 7 minutes. Fill jars and seal. Delicious!

HONEYED PORT JELLY

Yield: four 8-ounce jars

2½ cups honey
¾ cup port wine
3 ounces (½ bottle) liquid pectin
2 tablespoons lemon juice

Combine honey and wine; bring to a boil. Add pectin, stirring constantly. Return to a full rolling boil. Add lemon juice and remove from heat. Skim. Pour hot jelly into sterilized jars. Seal.

During the last 20 years, the number of honeybee colonies in the United States has declined at an average rate of 1 percent per year.

Vegetables

HONEY VEGETABLE PIQUANT

Yield: 5–6 servings

2 cups sliced carrots
2 cups sliced celery
1 cup water
6 small green onions, cut in 1-inch pieces
1 package (10 ounces) frozen peas
1 teaspoon salt
$\frac{1}{4}$ cup honey
$\frac{1}{4}$ cup vinegar
2 tablespoons soy sauce
2 tablespoons cornstarch
$\frac{1}{2}$ teaspoon ground ginger
$\frac{1}{4}$ cup cold water

Cook carrots and celery in 1 cup water until crisp-tender, about 10 minutes. Add green onions, peas, and salt; cook about 2 minutes. Combine honey, vinegar, and soy sauce and stir into vegetables. Bring to a boil. Mix cornstarch and ginger into $\frac{1}{4}$ cup cold water. Gradually add to vegetable mixture, stirring constantly. Add a little salt if needed. Cook a few minutes and serve at once.

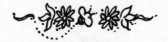

Pollen is carried back to the hive, where the bees store it as beebread in the cells of the honeycomb.

HONEY BEETS

Yield: 4 servings

3 cups diced, cooked beets
2 tablespoons butter
1 tablespoon grated orange peel
$1/4$ cup orange juice
$1/2$ cup honey
$1/2$ teaspoon salt
$1/2$ teaspoon pepper

Place beets in a heavy saucepan. Add all other ingredients. Cook over low heat, stirring constantly, until liquid has evaporated and honey forms a glaze over beets. Do not brown.

DEVILED CARROTS

Yield: 6 servings

$1/2$ cup butter
6 carrots, cut in strips
$1/4$ teaspoon salt
2 tablespoons honey
$1/2$ teaspoon dry mustard
$1/8$ teaspoon freshly ground pepper

In a large skillet, melt butter and add carrots. Add salt. Cover tightly and cook until tender (15 to 20 minutes). Combine honey, mustard, and ground pepper. Stir frequently to coat carrots evenly. Cook a few minutes and serve hot.

In 1967, an estimated 10 percent of the American bee population was seriously damaged or killed by insecticides.

CANDIED CARROTS AND GRAPES

Yield: 6 servings

$1/4$ cup butter
2 teaspoons cornstarch
honey
1 teaspoon lemon juice
$1/8$ teaspoon ground cinnamon
3 cups cooked carrots
1 cup green grapes, sliced

Melt butter; blend in cornstarch. Add honey, lemon juice, and cinnamon. Cook, stirring constantly, until mixture boils. Add glaze to carrots and grapes.

The Italian strain of honeybees is the most common in the United States. These bees are hardy, industrious, relatively gentle, and are yellow to brown in color. Caucasian bees are also widely kept. Bees in this strain are more gentle than Italian bees and gray to black in color.

GLAZED ONIONS OR CARROTS

Yield: 2 servings

1 cup small white onions or sliced carrots
4 tablespoons butter
$\frac{1}{4}$ cup honey

Cook onions or carrots in boiling salted water about 20–30 minutes, or until tender. Drain. Let stand a few minutes to dry. Melt butter in a saucepan. Add honey. Blend well, and then add onions or carrots and cook slowly until browned and well glazed. Turn vegetables occasionally for an even glaze.

A mouse that enters a hive looking for honey but pays with its life for its presumption is too large for the bees to carry out of the hive. To protect the hive from contamination, the workers seal the mouse in propolis or bee glue, a substance made from a brown resin they collect from trees. In the hot, dry air of the hive, the sealed corpse becomes mummified. In this preserved state, it is no longer a source of infection.

AMBER ONIONS

Yield: 8 servings

8 medium-sized white or yellow onions
1 teaspoon salt
$\frac{1}{2}$ teaspoon paprika
2 tablespoons melted butter
$\frac{1}{4}$ cup tomato juice
3 tablespoons honey

Cut onions in half crosswise. Place in a greased, large, shallow casserole. Combine salt, paprika, melted butter, tomato juice, and honey. Pour over onions. Cover dish and bake at 300 degrees for 60 minutes or until onions are tender. Serve with roasts or steaks.

HONEY SWEET POTATO BALLS

Yield: 8–10 servings

2 cups mashed sweet potatoes
honey
small marshmallows
corn flakes

Take a small amount of potatoes (approximately ¼ cup) and place a few marshmallows in the center; form into a ball. Roll the balls in crushed corn flakes. Place in a buttered baking dish and pour honey over top. Bake at 325 degrees for 30 minutes.

SPICED ACORN SQUASH

Yield: 4 servings

2 acorn squash
4 tablespoons butter
4 tablespoons honey
⅛ teaspoon ground cinnamon
salt to taste

Cut squash in half and remove seeds. Bake, cut side down, on a baking sheet, at 350 degrees for 30–45 minutes, until squash is tender. Turn halves up and sprinkle with salt. Divide the butter and honey equally among the four cavities; dust each with cinnamon. Bake 10 additional minutes.

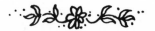

The queen lays her eggs in an area of the hive called the brood chamber. One square inch of the brood chamber contains about 28 small cells for eggs if they are destined to be workers or 18 larger cells for drones. Cells designed to rear a queen are the largest of all.

SPICED FROZEN SQUASH

Yield: 3–4 servings

1 package (12 ounces) frozen squash
salt to taste
3 tablespoons butter
3 tablespoons honey
$\frac{1}{8}$ teaspoon ground cinnamon

Cook squash according to package directions with salt and butter. Blend in honey and cinnamon and return to heat a minute or two.

BAKED BEANS PIZAZZ

Yield: 12–15 servings

1 medium onion, chopped
1 green pepper, chopped
1 clove garlic, minced
2 tablespoons vegetable oil
2 cans (1 pound, 12 ounces each) baked beans
$\frac{1}{2}$ cup ketchup
$\frac{1}{3}$ cup honey
hot red pepper sauce (optional)

Sauté onion, green pepper, and garlic in oil until soft but not brown. Combine with beans, ketchup, honey, and a few drops of hot pepper sauce, if desired, in a 2-quart casserole dish. Bake, uncovered, at 350 degrees for 1 to 2 hours.

> *The scout honeybee's "waggle" dance specifies the location of food. She traces a modified figure-eight pattern, vibrating her body as she reaches the intersection of the two halves.*

Breads and Cereals

TOOTSIE'S BANANA BREAD

Yield: 1 loaf

1³/₄ cups sifted unbleached flour
2 teaspoons baking powder
¹/₄ teaspoon baking soda
¹/₂ teaspoon salt
²/₃ cup honey
¹/₃ cup soft butter or shortening
2 eggs, unbeaten
¹/₂ cup chopped nuts
2 large or 3 small bananas, mashed (1 cup)

Grease a 9-by-5-by-3-inch loaf pan. Preheat oven to 350 degrees. In a large bowl, sift together flour, baking powder, baking soda, and salt. Add honey, butter, eggs, nuts, and mashed bananas. Beat together about 1 minute, scraping bowl. Pour into prepared pan and bake for 60 minutes.

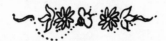

Bees have specially equipped rear legs designed for carrying pollen. They dust flower blossoms and scrape the pollen into sacs on the inside of their rear legs.

BANANA WALNUT BREAD

Yield: 1 loaf

$^1/_3$ cup butter or shortening
$^2/_3$ cup mild-flavored honey
2 eggs
3 tablespoons sour milk or buttermilk
1 cup mashed ripe bananas
2 cups whole wheat flour
1 teaspoon baking powder
$^1/_2$ teaspoon soda
$^1/_2$ teaspoon salt
$^1/_2$ cup finely chopped walnuts

Grease a 9-by-5-by-3-inch loaf pan. Cream butter or shortening until soft. Continue creaming while adding honey in a fine stream. Add eggs; beat well. Combine milk and mashed bananas in a separate bowl. Sift together dry ingredients. Add dry ingredients alternately with banana mixture to creamed mixture, beginning and ending with dry ingredients. Stir in nuts. Spoon into prepared pan. Let stand 15 minutes while oven preheats to 350 degrees. Bake 1 hour or until done in the center. Cool on rack 10 minutes. Remove from pan. Complete cooling on rack.

When measuring honey, heat the spoon in hot water and wipe it dry quickly before dipping it into the honey jar.

HONEY CARROT BREAD

Yield: 1 loaf

- 1 cup honey
- 1 tablespoon vegetable oil
- 1 cup finely grated raw carrots
- 1 cup hot water
- 2 eggs, lightly beaten
- 2½ cups whole wheat flour
- 1 teaspoon salt
- 2½ teaspoons baking powder
- ½ teaspoon baking soda
- 1 cup coarsely chopped walnuts

Grease a 9-by-5-by-3-inch loaf pan. In a large bowl, combine honey, oil, and carrots. Pour on hot water. Stir to mix, then cool. Add eggs. Combine flour, salt, baking powder, and soda. Fold into carrot mixture, mixing only until dry ingredients are moistened; do not beat. Stir in nuts. Pour batter into prepared pan. Let stand 5 minutes while preheating oven to 350 degrees. Bake 1 hour or until the loaf is done in the center. Cool on a rack 10 minutes; remove loaf from pan and continue to cool on the rack. When cool, wrap well in foil or plastic wrap and let stand in a cool place 12–24 hours before serving.

> *Bees can recognize polarized light, can sense temperature changes within ½ degree Fahrenheit, and have an incredible sense of time.*

HONEY-CRANBERRY BREAD

Yield: 2 loaves

6 cups commercial biscuit mix
1 teaspoon ground allspice
2 cups fresh cranberries, rinsed and drained
orange peel
1 cup chopped blanched almonds
2 eggs, well beaten
1 cup honey
$\frac{1}{2}$ cup milk
$\frac{1}{2}$ cup orange juice

Preheat oven to 350 degrees. Grease and flour two 9-by-5-by-3-inch loaf pans. Combine biscuit mix, allspice, cranberries, orange peel, and almonds. Add eggs, honey, milk, and orange juice; beat until well blended. Spoon into prepared pans. Bake 50–55 minutes or until loaves spring back when touched. Remove from pans and cool thoroughly on wire racks. Slice thinly to make sandwiches. (Suggested fillings: cream cheese and jelly, deviled ham and thinly sliced apple, or peanut butter and sliced bananas.)

> *A product called Baby Bees consists of mature bee pupae, rich in vitamins A and D.*

HONEY FLAKE MUFFINS

Yield: 10 medium-sized muffins

1 cup whole wheat flour
1 teaspoon salt
3 teaspoons baking powder
1 egg
$\frac{1}{4}$ cup honey
$\frac{1}{2}$ cup milk
4 tablespoons melted butter
2 cups wheat flakes or corn flakes

Grease the bottoms of ten 3-inch muffin cups. Preheat oven to 350 degrees. Stir flour, salt, and baking powder together. Beat egg until light; add honey and milk and stir into dry ingredients, being careful not to overmix. Add slightly cooled butter and stir just enough to mix ingredients. Carefully fold in cereal flakes. Fill muffin cups ²/₃ full. Bake about 25 minutes.

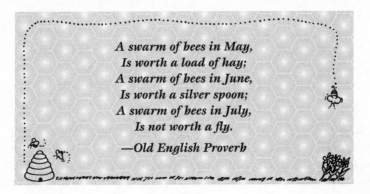

A swarm of bees in May,
Is worth a load of hay;
A swarm of bees in June,
Is worth a silver spoon;
A swarm of bees in July,
Is not worth a fly.

—Old English Proverb

DATE BRAN MUFFINS

Yield: 12 muffins

¹/₄ cup softened butter or shortening
¹/₄ cup honey
1 egg
³/₄ cup milk
1 cup whole bran
1 cup pitted dates, snipped
1 cup whole wheat flour
2 teaspoons baking powder
¹/₂ teaspoon salt

Grease the bottoms of 12 muffin cups. Preheat oven to 400 degrees. Cream together butter and honey. Add egg; beat well. Stir in milk, bran, and dates. In another bowl, stir together flour, baking powder, and salt. Add to batter. Stir just to moisten ingredients. Batter will look lumpy. Spoon into muffin cups, filling ²/₃ full. Bake 20 to 25 minutes or until done.

HONEY AND BISCUITS DELUXE

Yield: 2 ring cakes

DATE AND NUT MIXTURE

$^1/_2$ cup soft butter
$^1/_2$ cup honey
1 teaspoon cinnamon
$^1/_4$ cup chopped dates
$^1/_4$ cup coarsely chopped
    walnuts

HONEY BISCUIT MIX

$^1/_4$ cup soft butter
2 tablespoons honey
$^3/_4$ cup milk
3 cups biscuit mix

HONEY BUTTER GLAZE (OPTIONAL)

2 tablespoons soft butter
$^1/_4$ cup creamed-style honey

Preheat oven to 350 degrees. Prepare date and nut mixture by blending together $^1/_2$ cup soft butter with honey and cinnamon. Mix in dates and walnuts. Set aside. Prepare honey biscuit mix: In a mixing bowl, blend $^1/_4$ cup butter with 2 tablespoons of honey. Add milk and then biscuit mix. Using a fork, stir to form a soft dough. Butter two 9-inch ring molds. Drop dough by tablespoons into the ring molds, distributing dough evenly between the two molds. Lightly spread date and nut mixture over dough in rings. Bake about 35 minutes or until golden brown. Remove from the oven, let stand a couple of minutes, and then invert molds onto plates. After 5 minutes, remove molds. If desired, prepare honey butter glaze: Combine 2 tablespoons of butter with $^1/_4$ cup honey; spread lightly over warm coffee cake. Serve warm.

GRAHAM DATE BREAD

Yield: 1 loaf

$^1/_2$ cup whole wheat flour

$1^1/_2$ teaspoons baking powder

$^1/_2$ teaspoon salt

2 cups graham cracker crumbs (about 24 crackers)

1 cup chopped dates

$^3/_4$ cup chopped walnuts or almonds

$^1/_2$ cup shortening

$^1/_2$ cup honey

2 eggs

2 tablespoons grated orange peel

$^1/_3$ cup fresh orange juice

Grease bottom of 9-by-5-by-3-inch loaf pan and line with wax paper or aluminum foil; then grease again. Stir together flour, baking powder, and salt. Combine with graham cracker crumbs, dates, and nuts. Cream shortening. Continue creaming while adding honey slowly in a fine stream. Add eggs, one at a time, beating after each addition. Add date mixture alternately with combined orange peel and juice, mixing only until dry ingredients are dampened. Bake 50 to 60 minutes or until center is done. Cool 10 minutes before removing from pan. Cool completely before slicing with a sharp knife.

> *The owl and the pussycat went to sea*
> *in a beautiful pea-green boat.*
> *They took some honey and plenty of money*
> *wrapped up in a five-pound note.*
>
> —*Edward Lear*

ORANGE NUT BREAD

Yield: 1 loaf

1 cup honey
2 tablespoons shortening
1 egg, beaten
1½ tablespoons grated orange peel
¾ cup orange juice
2¼ cups whole wheat flour
2½ teaspoons baking powder
⅛ teaspoon baking soda
½ teaspoon salt
¾ cup chopped nuts

Grease a 9-by-5-by-3-inch loaf pan; line bottom with wax paper. Preheat oven to 325 degrees. Combine honey and shortening. Add egg and orange peel. Sift the dry ingredients and add alternately with the orange juice. Add chopped nuts. Pour into prepared pan. Bake for 1 hour or until the loaf is nicely browned.

NUTTY WHEAT BREAD

Yield: 1 loaf

2¼ cups whole wheat flour
1 teaspoon salt
½ teaspoon baking soda
2 teaspoons baking powder
1 cup coarsely chopped walnuts
2 eggs
⅔ cup honey
2 tablespoons vegetable oil or melted shortening
1 cup buttermilk

Preheat oven to 325 degrees. Grease and line a 9-by-5-by-3-inch loaf pan. Mix together flour, salt, soda, baking powder, and nuts. In a mixing bowl, beat eggs well. Add honey, oil, and buttermilk. Add dry ingredients, mixing only until blended. Spoon into prepared pan. Bake 50 to 60 minutes or until done in center. Cool on rack 10 minutes. Remove from pan. Complete cooling on rack.

Honey's ability to attract moisture is due to its potassium and levulose content.

HONEY ZUCCHINI BREAD

Yield: 2 loaves

3 cups whole wheat flour
1 teaspoon salt
1 teaspoon baking soda
$^1/_2$ teaspoon baking powder
1 tablespoon cinnamon
3 eggs
$^2/_3$ cup vegetable oil
$1^3/_4$ cups honey
1 tablespoon vanilla
2 cups finely grated, raw, unpeeled zucchini
1 cup finely chopped nuts

Grease and line with wax paper two $8^1/_2$-by-$4^1/_2$-inch loaf pans. Preheat oven to 325 degrees. In a large bowl, mix together dry ingredients. Set aside. In a medium bowl, mix together slightly beaten eggs, oil, honey, vanilla, and zucchini. Add to dry ingredients, stirring only enough to moisten. Do not beat. Add nuts. Pour into prepared pans, pushing batter into corners. Bake 1 hour or until bread is done in center. Cool on rack 10 minutes. Remove from pans. Complete cooling on rack. (Note: Sliced bread freezes well.)

Bees use the sun as a compass. When there is no sun, they fall back on the extensive patterns of polarized light in the sky. When clouds abbreviate these patterns, they rely on a third, noncelestial, reference system, the earth's magnetic field.

HONEY-ORANGE MUFFINS

Yield: 12 muffins

$1/2$ cup white flour
$1/2$ teaspoon salt
2 teaspoons baking powder
$1/2$ cup whole wheat flour
1 egg
$1/4$ cup orange juice
1 teaspoon grated orange peel
$1/2$ cup honey
3 tablespoons melted butter or shortening

Grease the bottoms of 12 muffin cups. Preheat oven to 400 degrees. Sift white flour with salt and baking powder; stir in whole wheat flour. Combine egg, orange juice, peel, honey, and butter. Add all at once to flour. Pour batter into prepared muffin pan, filling cups $2/3$ full. Bake 15–20 minutes.

HONEY-BLUEBERRY MUFFINS

Yield: 12 muffins

2 cups whole wheat flour
1 teaspoon salt
3 teaspoons baking powder
$1/2$ cup fresh blueberries
1 cup milk
4 tablespoons honey
1 egg, beaten
$1/4$ cup melted butter or shortening

Preheat oven to 400 degrees; grease the bottoms of 12 muffin cups. Combine flour with salt and baking powder; add blueberries. Mix milk, honey, egg, and melted butter or shortening. Add to dry mixture. Stir quickly, just enough to moisten dry ingredients. Fill prepared muffin cups $2/3$ full; bake 25–30 minutes or until delicately browned.

> *To provide Americans with one year's supply of honey,*
> *honeybees must travel 10,141,440,000,000 miles.*

FRUITED HONEY MUFFINS

Yield: 18 muffins

1 cup whole bran cereal
1 cup raisins
1 cup honey
1 cup milk
1¼ cups whole wheat flour
2 teaspoons baking powder
2 teaspoons cinnamon
⅛ teaspoon nutmeg
2 eggs, slightly beaten
¼ cup vegetable oil
1 tablespoon grated lemon peel
1 cup finely chopped nuts (optional)

Grease well 18 large muffin cups. Preheat oven to 400 degrees. In a large bowl, combine cereal, raisins, honey, and milk. Set aside. Mix together flour, baking powder, and spices. Fold eggs and oil into bran mixture. Stir in dry ingredients until moistened, but do not beat. Add lemon peel and nuts. Fill muffin cups ⅔ full. Bake 20 minutes or until done. Loosen edges of muffins with spatula. Serve hot. (Note: These freeze well.)

> *The queen bee can lay up to 2,000 eggs per day.*

CORN STICKS

Yield: 36 small corn sticks

2$\frac{1}{2}$ teaspoons baking powder
1 teaspoon salt
1$\frac{1}{4}$ cups sifted flour
1 cup corn meal
2 eggs, well beaten
1$\frac{1}{4}$ cups milk
3 tablespoons honey
$\frac{1}{4}$ cup melted shortening

Preheat oven to 425 degrees. Grease corn stick pans. Add baking powder and salt to sifted flour and sift again. Add corn meal and mix well. Combine eggs, milk, honey, and melted shortening. Add to dry ingredients; mix well. Bake in prepared pans for 25 minutes, or until done.

> *Store honey at room temperature—not in the refrigerator. Keep the container closed and in a dry place.*

POPOVERS

Yield: 6–8 popovers

1 cup flour
$\frac{1}{2}$ teaspoon salt
$\frac{3}{4}$ cup milk
2 tablespoons honey
1 tablespoon melted butter
2 large eggs

Grease 8 muffin cups. Preheat oven to 300 degrees. Sift flour and salt. Add milk, honey, and butter. Blend. Beat in eggs. Fill muffin cups just half full. Bake 25 to 30 minutes. Do not open oven door or popovers will fall. Serve with marmalade, honey, or honey butter.

HONEY WHOLE WHEAT WAFFLES

Yield: 10–12 waffles

2 cups whole wheat flour
3 teaspoons baking powder
1 teaspoon salt
1 large egg, beaten
$\frac{1}{4}$ cup melted butter
3 tablespoons honey
2 cups milk

Combine flour, baking powder, and salt. Mix butter and honey with beaten egg. Stir flour and milk into egg mixture. Beat until smooth. Bake in hot waffle iron. Serve with Honey Butter (page 121).

The worker bee's stinging mechanism is a tiny precision instrument made up of no fewer than 20 different parts.

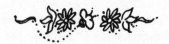

HONEY FRENCH TOAST

Yield: 4–6 servings

2 eggs, slightly beaten
$\frac{1}{4}$ cup milk
$\frac{1}{4}$ cup honey
$\frac{1}{4}$ teaspoon salt
8 slices bread
butter

TOPPING
1 cup honey
2 tablespoons lemon juice
2 tablespoons butter

Combine beaten eggs, $\frac{1}{4}$ cup milk, $\frac{1}{4}$ cup honey, and salt; dip bread in mixture and fry in butter until golden brown. To make topping, combine remaining honey, lemon juice, and 2 tablespoons butter. Heat and serve over toast.

*Bees can learn a flower's color only in the few seconds
before they land, although they continue to see it
during feeding and departure.*

UNEXPECTED COMPANY

Yield: 3 cups

4 tablespoons butter
4 tablespoons whole wheat flour
1 cup tomato juice
1 cup milk
1 1/2 cups cottage cheese
honeyed toast

Melt butter. Blend in flour. Stir in tomato juice and milk. Add cottage cheese. Stir until thickened and smooth. Serve on crisp toast, lightly spread with honey.

*The hexagonal shape of honeycomb cells is one
of the most efficient means of storing cylindrical
objects within a confined area.*

BEEHIVE BREAD

Yield: 1 loaf

3 cups whole wheat flour
1 teaspoon salt
1 package active dry yeast
1 tablespoon grated orange peel
1/2 cup milk
3 tablespoons butter
1/4 cup water
1/2 cup honey

In a large bowl, mix 3/4 cup flour with salt, yeast, and orange peel. Combine milk, butter, water, and honey in a saucepan; heat until warm. Gradually add liquid to dry ingredients and beat about 2 minutes. Add remaining flour. Shape dough in a ball; place in a lightly greased bowl, turning to coat evenly; and leave to rise in a warm place until doubled, about 1¼ hours. Preheat oven to 350 degrees. Punch down and shape in a rectangular or round loaf. Place in a lightly greased 9-by-5-by-3-inch loaf pan or place round loaf in a greased 2-quart round casserole dish. Bake about 60 minutes.

In addition to its sugars, honey contains minerals, seven members of the B-vitamin complex, ascorbic acid (vitamin C), dextrins, plant pigments, amino acids, traces of protein, esters and other aromatic compounds, and several enzymes.

OLD-TIME BISCUIT BREAD

Yield: 2 loaves

1 cup shredded wheat crumbs
3 cups boiling water
2 tablespoons vegetable oil
1 tablespoon salt
½ cup mild-flavored honey
2 cakes compressed yeast or 2 packages active dry yeast
¼ cup lukewarm water
about 7 cups whole wheat flour

Grease 2 loaf pans, 9-by-5-by-3-inch. In a large bowl, mix 1 cup shredded wheat crumbs with boiling water, oil, salt, and honey. Cool. Blend yeast with lukewarm water. Stir into cooled biscuit mixture. Add flour in three parts, beating until dough is of handling consistency (it will be soft). Turn dough onto lightly floured board. Knead until elastic, about 5 minutes. Place in a greased bowl, turning to grease top. Cover, let rise in a warm place until double in bulk, about 2 hours. Divide into two equal parts. Shape into loaves and place in prepared pans. Cover. Let rise until doubled in size, about 1 hour. Preheat oven to 350 degrees. Bake 45–50 minutes or until done. Remove from pans. Brush tops with butter. Cool on wire rack.

In ancient Egypt, honey was offered to the gods, buried in tombs with the dead to provide food in the hereafter, and given to newborn babies to ward off evil spirits and to bestow gifts of health, poetic inspiration, and eloquence. Almost all Egyptian medicines contained honey. Honey unearthed 33 centuries after it was buried in the tombs of Egypt was found to be edible when taken from the jars.

HONEY GRANOLA LOAF

Yield: 2 loaves

$6^1/_4$–$6^3/_4$ cups whole wheat flour
2 packages active dry yeast
1 tablespoon salt
$1^1/_4$ cups water
1 cup milk
$^1/_2$ cup honey
$^1/_4$ cup shortening
2 eggs
2 cups granola, any flavor, crushed

In a large mixing bowl, combine 3 cups flour, yeast, and salt. Mix well. In a saucepan, heat water, milk, honey, and shortening until warm, or 120 to 130 degrees (shortening does not need to melt). Add to flour mixture. Add eggs. Blend at low speed until moistened; beat 3 minutes at medium speed. By hand, gradually stir in granola and enough remaining flour to make a firm dough. Knead on a floured surface until smooth and elastic, about 8–10 minutes. Place in a greased bowl, turning to grease top. Cover and let rise in a warm place until light and doubled, about $1^1/_2$ hours.

Punch down dough. Divide dough in half, and then each half into three pieces. Roll each piece on lightly floured surface to make a 14-inch rope. Place ropes together side by side; pinch tops together and loosely braid. Pinch ends and tuck under to seal. Place in 2 greased 9-by-5-inch pans. Cover. Let rise in warm place until light and doubled, about 1 hour. Bake for 30 to 35 minutes until golden brown and loaves sound hollow when tapped. Cover loosely with foil the last 5 to 10 minutes of baking. Remove from pans. Cool.

> *The hexagonal wax cells in the honeycomb are from*
> *$1/280$ to $1/500$ inch thick. The structure is built with*
> *incredible efficiency, with a minimum expenditure of*
> *materials, and in a very short time. And it's all done*
> *without the use of a single instrument!*

CRUSTY OATMEAL BREAD

Yield: 1 loaf

$3^{1}/_{2}$ cups whole wheat flour
1 package active dry yeast
$^{1}/_{2}$ cup milk
$^{1}/_{2}$ cup water
$^{1}/_{2}$ cup butter
$^{1}/_{4}$ cup honey
1 teaspoon salt
2 eggs
1 cup oats

Grease a 2-quart casserole dish or a 9-by-5-inch loaf pan. Stir together 2 cups flour and yeast in a large mixing bowl. Heat milk, water, butter, honey, and salt over low heat only until warm, stirring to blend. Add liquid ingredients to flour and yeast mixture and beat until smooth, about 2 minutes. Blend in eggs and oats. Add remaining flour and beat 1 minute. Cover with damp towel and let rise in warm place until double in volume, about 1 hour. Preheat oven to 375 degrees. Stir down. Pour batter in prepared pan. Bake for 55 to 60 minutes. Cool 10 minutes on rack before removing from pan. Brush top of loaf with melted butter.

Honeybees are not "plunderers" of food from the flowers. They reciprocate and perform a service for the plants by effecting pollination.

HONEY-OATMEAL BREAD

Yield: 2 loaves

1 cup boiling water
1 cup rolled oats
1/3 cup soft shortening
1/3 cup honey
1 tablespoon salt
2 packages active dry yeast
1 cup warm water
1 egg
4–5 cups whole wheat flour

Grease 2 loaf pans, 9-by-5-by-3-inch. Stir the boiling water, oats, shortening, honey, and salt together in a large mixing bowl. Cool to lukewarm. Dissolve yeast in 1 cup warm water. Add dissolved yeast and water, egg, and 2 cups of flour to the oat mixture. Beat 2 minutes at medium speed with mixer or by hand until batter is smooth. By hand, gradually stir in remaining flour to make a stiff batter. Spread batter evenly in prepared pans. Smooth tops of loaves by patting into shape. Cover and let rise in warm place about 1½ hours. Preheat oven to 375 degrees and bake 50–55 minutes. Remove from pans and brush with melted butter.

CASSEROLE HONEY RYE BREAD

Yield: 1 round loaf

3$\frac{1}{2}$–4 cups whole wheat flour
1$\frac{1}{2}$ cups rye flour
2 packages active dry yeast
2 teaspoons caraway seeds
1 tablespoon salt
1 cup milk
1 cup water
$\frac{1}{2}$ cup honey
3 tablespoons shortening
1 egg

In a large mixer bowl, combine 1 cup whole wheat flour, all of the rye flour, yeast, 1 teaspoon caraway seeds, and salt. Mix well. In a saucepan, heat milk, water, honey, and shortening until warm. Add to flour mixture. Add egg. Blend at low speed until moistened; beat 3 minutes at medium speed. By hand, gradually stir in remaining wheat flour and make a stiff dough. Cover and let rise 50 minutes or until doubled. Turn dough into a well-greased 1$\frac{1}{2}$-quart casserole. Brush lightly with oil and sprinkle with remaining caraway seeds. Let rise about 30 minutes. Then bake in a preheated 375-degree oven for 40–45 minutes.

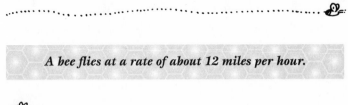

A bee flies at a rate of about 12 miles per hour.

WHOLE WHEAT BREAD

Yield: 2 loaves

> 1 package active dry yeast or 1 cake compressed yeast
> 1 cup water
> ½ cup honey
> 3 tablespoons shortening
> 1 tablespoon salt
> 1 cup milk
> 5½ cups whole wheat flour
> raisins (optional)

Soften yeast in ¼ cup warm water. Combine honey, shortening, and salt. Scald milk and add to honey mixture. Add ¾ cup cold water when liquid is lukewarm. If you wish to use raisins, put them in with the ¾ cup of cold water. Add softened yeast. Gradually add flour. Knead until smooth and satiny, about 7 to 10 minutes. Place in a greased bowl. Cover and let rise in a warm place until doubled, about 2 hours. Punch down, divide loaf into two halves. Shape in two loaves. Place in well-greased 9-by-5-by-3-inch loaf pans. Let rise in a warm place until doubled again. Bake at 350 degrees for 50 to 60 minutes. Remove from pans. Butter tops of loaves.

> *Worker bees collect pollen primarily to provide protein for the growing larvae.*

HONEY DATE ROLLS

Yield: 36 rolls

2 cups bran flakes
³/₄ cup dates, pitted
¹/₂ cup pecans
2 tablespoons honey
1 tablespoon butter
2 teaspoons lemon juice

Put bran flakes, dates, and nut meats through a meat grinder. Add honey, butter, and lemon juice. Knead mixture until well blended. Shape into 1-inch rolls or fingers and dust with confectioners' sugar.

MOUNTAIN GRANOLA

Yield: 11 cups

6 cups quick-cooking oats
1 cup shredded coconut
1 cup wheat germ
¹/₂ cup shelled sunflower seeds
³/₄ cup halved cashews
¹/₂ cup vegetable oil
¹/₂ cup honey
1–3 cups water as needed
1¹/₂ teaspoons salt
1¹/₂ teaspoons vanilla extract
1 cup raisins
1 cup dried apricots, chopped
1 cup dates, chopped

In a large bowl, combine oats, coconut, wheat germ, sunflower seeds, and cashews. Mix together oil, honey, water, salt, and vanilla. (Start with 1 cup water; if mixture is too dry, add more water as needed.) Pour over oatmeal mixture and stir until coated. Bake at 350 degrees for 30 minutes, stirring frequently. Cool and add fruit. Store in an airtight container. Granola has 500 calories per cup.

HONEY GRANOLA

Yield: 10 cups

4 cups oatmeal
$2^{1}/_{2}$ cups wheat germ
1 cup sunflower seeds
1 cup sesame seeds
1 cup unsweetened coconut
1 cup raw peanuts
2 teaspoons ground cinnamon
$^{3}/_{4}$ cup honey
$^{1}/_{2}$ cup vegetable oil
1 cup raisins (optional)

Mix dry ingredients in a large bowl. Heat together honey and oil; pour slowly over dry ingredients, mixing thoroughly. Bake in shallow pans at 325 degrees for 30 minutes, stirring every 10 minutes. Remove from oven. Add 1 cup raisins, if desired, and mix well.

Meats

LONDON BROIL

Yield: 6 servings

¹/₄ cup honey	6 London broil steaks
1 cup vinegar	salt
1 cup water	2 tablespoons honey
2 bay leaves	2 tablespoons flour
¹/₂ teaspoon peppercorns	¹/₄ teaspoon ground ginger
¹/₂ medium-sized onion, thinly sliced	1 cup sour cream

In a saucepan, combine honey, vinegar, water, bay leaves, peppercorns, and onions. Bring to a boil. Arrange London broil steaks in a pan for marinating. Pour hot vinegar mixture over steaks. Cover and refrigerate 12–24 hours, turning meat once. To cook, remove steaks from marinade and season with salt to taste. Brush cooking side of each steak with ¹/₂ teaspoon honey. Broil or cook on outdoor grill 4–5 minutes on first side. Brush other side with remaining honey and cook about 3 minutes. While steaks are cooking, make a sauce with 1 cup marinade, removing peppercorns and bay leaves. Blend in the flour, ginger, and a dash of salt. Cook and stir until it thickens. Fold in sour cream and heat until hot, but do not boil. Serve steaks topped with sauce.

Over 2 million bee journeys are required to make 1 pound of honey!

MARINATED FLANK STEAK

Yield: 10–12 servings

¼ cup soy sauce
3 tablespoons honey
2 tablespoons red wine vinegar
1½ teaspoons garlic powder
1½ teaspoons ground ginger
¾ cup vegetable oil
1 green onion, finely chopped
two 1½-pound flank steaks

Combine soy sauce, honey, and vinegar; add garlic powder, ginger, oil, and onion. Mix well. Cut excess fat from meat. Diagonally slash lightly, forming diamond patterns on meat surface, both sides. Place meat in a pan just large enough to hold it. Pour marinade over and allow to stand 4 hours at room temperature or overnight in the refrigerator, covered. Remove meat from marinade when ready to cook. Grill over medium-hot coals or broil to desired doneness, about 6 minutes per side for medium-rare. Slice thinly, on diagonal, to serve.

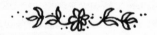

HONEY POT ROAST

Yield: 6–8 servings

3¹⁄₂–4 pounds chuck, blade, or other pot roast
¹⁄₂ package (2 tablespoons) onion soup mix
3 tablespoons water or dry red wine
¹⁄₂ cup tomato juice
2 tablespoons honey
1 bay leaf

Preheat oven to 325 degrees. Place roast in the center of a wide piece of heavy-duty aluminum foil in a roasting pan. Bring the foil up around the sides of the roast. Mix together onion soup and wine; stir in tomato juice and honey. Blend and pour over roast. Add bay leaf. Wrap foil loosely around meat, sealing edges to form an airtight package. Bake 45 minutes per pound. Skim off fat if necessary before thickening meat juices for gravy.

A majority of the eggs laid by the queen have been fertilized by sperm that the queen receives from one or more drones on her mating flights. She stores the sperm for use all through her life. The fertilized eggs develop into either workers or queens. In the summer, she also lays some unfertilized eggs, which develop into drones.

BEEF LOAF IN THE ROUND

Yield: 6 servings

$^3/_4$ cup milk
1 envelope (1$^3/_8$ ounces) onion soup mix
1 egg, lightly beaten
1$^1/_2$ cups soft breadcrumbs
1$^1/_2$ pounds lean ground beef
$^1/_4$ cup ketchup
1 tablespoon prepared mustard
2 tablespoons honey
4 slices Monterey Jack cheese

In a large mixing bowl, combine milk, soup mix, egg, and bread-crumbs. Let stand 5 minutes. Add ground beef and mix well. Shape mixture into 9-inch ring mold; then turn it out into a shallow baking pan. Blend ketchup with mustard and honey; brush ring. Bake 40 minutes in a 400-degree oven, basting occasionally with ketchup mixture. Remove ring from oven and arrange cheese slices over ring. Return to oven. Bake about 5 minutes, until cheese melts. Serve with cooked noodles or rice.

SAUCY MEAT LOAF

Yield: 6 servings

SAUCE
1 can (8 ounces)
   tomato sauce
2 tablespoons honey
1$^1/_2$ tablespoons vinegar
$^1/_2$ clove garlic, finely minced
1 green onion, thinly sliced
few drops red pepper sauce

MEAT LOAF
1 egg
$^1/_4$ cup milk
1$^1/_4$ teaspoons salt
$^1/_4$ teaspoon paprika
$^1/_8$ teaspoon pepper
$^1/_2$ cup dry, fine breadcrumbs
1 pound ground chuck
   or round

Combine sauce ingredients in a small saucepan. Bring to a boil and simmer 5 minutes. While sauce is cooking, combine meat loaf ingredients, mixing well. Spoon 3 tablespoons of sauce into the bottom of an 8-by-4-by-2-inch loaf pan. Spoon meat into pan and press into loaf shape. Bake at 350 degrees for 45–50 minutes.

For individual loaves, spoon 1 teaspoon of sauce into bottoms of six 3-inch muffin cups and divide meat evenly among cups, shaping to resemble muffins. Bake at 350 degrees for 25 minutes. Serve hot with additional sauce.

> *Some of the diseases that afflict honeybees are American foulbrood (AFB), European foulbrood (EFB), sacbrood, and nosema.*

SMOOTH CHILI CON CARNE

Yield: 4–6 servings

1 pound ground beef
1 cup chopped onions
1 cup diced celery
1 quart cooked or canned red beans
2 cups tomato puree
2 cups water
1 tablespoon salt
1 teaspoon chili powder
$1/3$ cup honey

Sauté beef, onions, and celery slowly until meat is done and vegetables are tender. Place beans, tomato puree, water, and salt in a large saucepan or Dutch oven. Bring mixture to a boil, and add meat and vegetables. Simmer slowly for 2 hours. Add chili powder; just before serving, stir in honey.

> *Numerous murals in ancient Egyptian graves depict honeybees.*

TOTE'N BEAN CASSEROLE

Yield: 10 servings

1 pound lean ground beef
$1/2$ pound bacon, cut in small pieces
1 cup chopped onions
2 cans (15 ounces each) pork and beans
1 can (16 ounces) kidney beans, drained
1 can (16 ounces) butter lima beans, drained
1 cup ketchup
$1/4$ cup honey
1 tablespoon liquid smoke
3 tablespoons wine vinegar
1 teaspoon salt
$1/2$ teaspoon pepper

Brown ground beef in a skillet; drain and place in a large casserole. Brown bacon and onions; drain. Add bacon and onions to casserole. Combine remaining ingredients; then stir into mixture in casserole. Bake at 300 degrees for 2 hours, stirring the first hour.

Note: This is a great recipe for a slow cooker. Prepare in the same manner. Cover and cook on low for 4 to 9 hours. Do not stir after the first hour.

> *The indiscriminate use of insecticides to control insect pests has killed off most of the wild bees that formerly pollinated crops across the nation. Many farmers rent colonies of bees to aid in the pollination of their crops.*

HOT DOG–BEAN COOKOUT

Yield: 8 servings

BAKED BEANS
1/4 cup honey
2 tablespoons instant
onion flakes
1/4 cup ketchup
1 can (16 ounces) pork
and beans

HOT DOGS WITH SAUCE
2 tablespoons butter,
margarine, or shortening
1 tablespoon soy sauce
1 teaspoon prepared mustard
1/2 cup honey
1 tablespoon vinegar
1 teaspoon cornstarch
8 hot dogs
8 hamburger buns

Prepare baked beans by combining ingredients in a casserole dish and baking at 350 degrees for 25 minutes. Prepare sauce for hot dogs by combining butter, soy sauce, mustard, honey, vinegar, and cornstarch in a saucepan. Simmer sauce 8–10 minutes until smooth and thick. Cut each hot dog halfway through in several places on one side only. Place on a baking sheet and grill, basting with sauce several times, until hot dogs form a circle. Place hot dogs on buns, filling centers with baked beans.

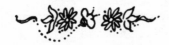

Beehives have an air-conditioning system whereby the bees effectively control the temperature and humidity—regardless of outside conditions. The inside temperature is a steady 95 degrees Fahrenheit.

APPLESAUCE PORK CHOPS

Yield: 6 servings

6 pork chops
salt and pepper
1 cup applesauce
1/4 cup honey
1 teaspoon lemon juice
1/4 teaspoon ground nutmeg
1/4 teaspoon ground cinnamon

Slash fat around chops and season with salt and pepper. Arrange on a rack in shallow pan and bake, uncovered, at 350 degrees for 30–45 minutes, or until tender. Drain fat from pan. Turn chops over and place them in the bottom of the pan. Combine applesauce, honey, lemon juice, and spices. Spoon over meat and return to oven. Reduce temperature to 300 degrees and bake an additional 15 to 20 minutes.

HONEY AND FRUIT PORK CHOPS

Yield: 4 servings

4 double-loin pork chops
1 can (8 1/2 ounces) sliced pineapple
1/2 cup honey
1/4 cup pineapple syrup (reserved from can)
1 tablespoon prepared mustard
4 maraschino cherries

Cut a pocket into each chop. Drain pineapple, reserving juice, and insert 1/2 slice of pineapple in each chop pocket. Combine honey, pineapple syrup, and mustard; spoon a little over each chop. Bake at 350 degrees for 1 1/2 hours, drizzling honey sauce over the chops frequently. Remove chops from the oven; top each with 1/2 slice of pineapple and a maraschino cherry. Return to oven for a minute or two to warm the fruit. Heat remaining honey sauce and serve with chops.

SWEET AND SOUR PINEAPPLE PORK

Yield: 4–6 servings

1 can (13 ounces) pineapple chunks
$^1\!/_2$ cup whole wheat flour
$^1\!/_2$ teaspoon monosodium glutamate
$^1\!/_2$ teaspoon salt
1 pound lean pork, cut in $^3\!/_4$-inch squares
1 egg, lightly beaten
2–4 tablespoons vegetable oil
$^1\!/_2$ cup honey
$^1\!/_3$ cup vinegar
2 teaspoons soy sauce
$^1\!/_3$ cup pineapple syrup (reserved from can)
$^1\!/_4$ cup ketchup
2 tablespoons cornstarch
$^1\!/_4$ cup water
1 medium-sized green pepper cut in thin strips
cooked rice or crisp noodles

Drain pineapple chunks and reserve syrup. Combine flour, mono-sodium glutamate, and salt. Dip pork cubes into beaten egg and then into seasoned flour. Cook in hot oil about 5 minutes or until crispy on all sides. Remove from pan and keep warm. In a saucepan, combine honey, vinegar, soy sauce, pineapple syrup, and ketchup, and bring to a boil. Mix cornstarch in water and add to sauce, stirring constantly. Cook until thickened. Add the cooked pork, pineapple chunks, and green pepper strips. Simmer for 5 minutes. Serve hot over steamed rice or crisp noodles.

> *It takes 556 worker bees flying 35,584 miles*
> *to produce 1 pound of honey!*

PORK CHOPS SUPREME

Yield: 6 servings

1 cup hot ketchup
6 tablespoons honey
6 pork chops, $1/2$ inch thick
1 large lemon, sliced

Blend ketchup and honey; pour over pork chops. Top each chop with a slice of fresh lemon. Bake uncovered at 325 degrees for 60 minutes or until done. (This sauce is also delicious over chicken pieces.)

The Indians of North America thought the honeybees that came with the European settlers brought misfortune and called them "white men's flies," for the arrival of the bees meant the arrival of the settlers.

HONEY 'N' WINE RIBS

Yield: 6–8 servings

4 pounds short ribs or spare ribs
1 can (8 ounces) tomato sauce
$1/4$ cup red wine
$1/2$ cup honey
$1/4$ cup red wine vinegar
1 tablespoon instant minced onion
1 teaspoon salt
1 teaspoon onion salt
1 teaspoon garlic salt
$1/8$ teaspoon ground cloves

Broil ribs under broiler for 30 minutes, turning occasionally, to brown and remove excess fat. Place ribs in a casserole dish. Combine remaining ingredients and pour over ribs. Cover casserole and bake in a 325-degree oven for approximately 60 minutes.

HONEY GLAZE FOR HAM

Bake ham according to package directions. When the ham is fully cooked, remove it from the oven and score the fat in a diamond pattern. Place ¼ of a maraschino cherry in each point or in the center of each diamond. Pour 1 cup of honey over the scored ham, using more honey if necessary to cover the ham uniformly. Return ham to hot oven for 15–20 minutes to brown the glaze.

ORANGE-HONEY GLAZE FOR HAM

1 can (6 ounces) frozen orange juice
1¾ cups water
¾ cup honey
1 teaspoon salt
1 tablespoon cornstarch

Place orange juice, water, honey, and salt in a saucepan. Blend cornstarch with ¼ cup of the mixture and add to pan. Cook, stirring constantly, until thick, about 3 minutes. Cool. Brush on cooked ham. Return to oven for 15 minutes.

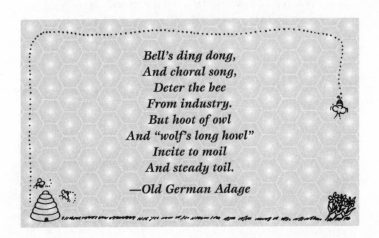

Bell's ding dong,
And choral song,
Deter the bee
From industry.
But hoot of owl
And "wolf's long howl"
Incite to moil
And steady toil.

—Old German Adage

> *Because of its ability to absorb and hold moisture,*
> *honey can help prevent bedwetting if given*
> *to children at bedtime.*

HONEYED CHICKEN

Yield: 4 servings

>   1 broiler-fryer (3–4 pounds), quartered
>   melted butter
>   ¹/₂ cup honey
>   2 tablespoons soy sauce

Arrange chicken in a shallow baking pan. Brush with melted butter. Combine honey with soy sauce and brush over chicken. Bake at 350 degrees for about 1¹/₂ hours, brushing frequently with honey sauce. If desired, thicken remaining sauce with cornstarch and pour over chicken.

> *When a bee is collecting nectar, it will usually*
> *concentrate on one species of flower at a time.*

CHINESE CHICKEN

Yield: 4 servings

>   1 frying chicken (3 pounds), cut up
>   1 egg
>   2 tablespoons vegetable oil or melted shortening
>   2 tablespoons lemon juice
>   2 tablespoons soy sauce
>   ¹/₄ cup honey
>   1 tablespoon paprika
>   1 teaspoon salt
>   pepper (optional)

Arrange chicken pieces in a single layer in a baking pan. Beat egg lightly; add remaining ingredients and mix well. Pour sauce over chicken, turning pieces to coat. Bake uncovered at 325 degrees for 60 minutes, basting once with sauce. For a crisp top, run under broiler. Serve hot or cold.

HONEY LEMON CHICKEN

Yield: 6 servings

$2^{1}/_{2}$–3 pounds chicken pieces (12 pieces)
$^{1}/_{3}$ cup flour
1 teaspoon paprika
1 teaspoon salt
$^{1}/_{3}$ cup butter
$^{1}/_{3}$ cup honey
$^{1}/_{4}$ cup lemon juice

Combine flour, paprika, and salt; roll chicken in mixture. Melt butter and coat floured chicken pieces well. Bake at 375 degrees for 45 minutes. Combine honey and lemon juice; brush or pour over hot chicken to glaze. Return chicken to oven for 15 minutes at 350 degrees.

In each of its two eyes, a queen bee has from 3,000 to 4,000 facets, a worker from 4,000 to 5,000, and a drone from 7,000 to 8,000 facets. Yet a bee can only see the rough outlines of its environment.

*Drones (male bees) live from late spring
until the end of summer.*

MOON GLOW CHICKEN

Yield: 6 servings

3 pounds chicken pieces
³/₄ cup orange juice
2 tablespoons lemon juice
¹/₄ cup vegetable oil
¹/₄ cup honey
1 teaspoon salt
¹/₂ teaspoon pepper
1 teaspoon dry mustard or curry powder
¹/₂ teaspoon paprika

Combine all ingredients except chicken and shake or blend until well mixed. In a large bowl, place chicken pieces skin side down. Pour sauce over the chicken and rotate pieces to coat completely. Cover bowl and marinate in refrigerator for several hours or overnight. Remove chicken from sauce and place, skin side down, on a rack in a roasting pan. Baste chicken with sauce. Bake at 400 degrees for 30 minutes. Turn chicken and baste with remaining sauce. Bake 30 minutes more until done.

Note: If chicken browns too fast, cover with foil. If desired, recipe may be halved and cooked in a skillet.

*Each beehive has its own scent—the scent of the queen.
A bee rarely returns to the wrong hive.*

HONEY-PECAN HAM GLAZE

1 cup honey
2 teaspoons dry mustard
$^1/_2$ teaspoon ground cloves
$^1/_2$ teaspoon ground cinnamon
pecan halves

Combine ingredients. Pour $^1/_3$ of glaze over hot, baked ham and return to oven for 10 minutes. Pour remaining glaze over at 10-minute intervals, $^1/_3$ each time. Remove from oven. Arrange pecan halves over top and return to oven for 5 more minutes.

HONEY LEMON PRECARVED LAMB SHOULDER

Yield: 8 servings

shoulder of lamb
$^1/_4$ cup chopped parsley
salt and pepper
1 lemon, sliced
$^1/_3$ cup honey
2 tablespoons orange juice
$^1/_8$ teaspoon ground allspice

Have butcher saw and tie lamb shoulder. Sprinkle parsley, salt, and pepper on and in carved lamb. Place on a rack in a shallow roasting pan and roast at 325 degrees for 30–35 minutes per pound. Half an hour before lamb is done, halve lemon slices and insert in lamb. Blend honey, orange juice, and allspice and baste lamb two or three times during the last 30 minutes of roasting.

All honey-gathering worker bees are female.

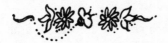

LUAU LAMB

Yield: 6–8 servings

2 pounds boneless lamb shoulder
pineapple chunks
green pepper slices
mushrooms
$^1/_2$ cup honey
1 cup pineapple juice
3 tablespoons butter or margarine
1 teaspoon Worcestershire sauce
1 teaspoon prepared mustard
1 teaspoon garlic salt
$^1/_4$ teaspoon ground ginger
2 tablespoons chopped mint leaves (optional)

Cut lamb in $1^1/_2$-inch cubes. Arrange meat, pineapple chunks, green pepper slices, and mushrooms on skewers. Combine remaining ingredients and simmer in a saucepan for 10 minutes. Brush generously over kabobs. Grill for 15 to 20 minutes, or until tender, turning often and basting with sauce. Serve on fluffy seasoned rice.

HONEY-GLAZED DUCKLING

Yield: 4 servings

5-pound duckling
1 teaspoon salt
1 teaspoon seasoned salt
1 teaspoon poultry seasoning
$^1/_2$ teaspoon paprika
$^1/_2$ cup honey
$^1/_3$ cup orange-flavored liqueur or lemon juice
$1^1/_2$ teaspoons dry mustard
5 thin slices lemon
5 thin slices onion

Clean duck and prick skin to allow fat to drain off when cooking. Combine salt, seasoned salt, poultry seasoning, and paprika; rub inside and outside of duck. Place duck in a 450-degree oven for 15 minutes; drain off fat. Reduce oven to 350 degrees and bake for 1 hour, draining off fat as necessary. Combine honey, liqueur, and mustard; brush duck with mixture. Secure sliced lemon and onion onto duck with toothpicks and continue to bake for 45 minutes, brushing occasionally with honey glaze. (Apple slices or bread can be stuffed inside duck to help soak up fat; remove them after baking.)

> *The haven of the ancient Israelites was the*
> *Promised Land of milk and honey.*

CURRY KABOBS

Yield: *⅓ cup sauce*

CURRY SAUCE
2 tablespoons butter
½ teaspoon hot Cantonese or Dijon mustard
¼ cup honey
1 tablespoon soy sauce
¾ teaspoon curry powder

KABOB SUGGESTIONS
Fruits: apple wedges, maraschino cherries, unpeeled orange
    wedges, pineapple cubes
Meats (cubes or wedges): bologna, tender beef or lamb,
    Canadian bacon, canned meat, precooked ham, Vienna
    sausage, wieners
Vegetables (cubes, slices, or small whole): eggplant,
    mushrooms, cooked onions, green peppers, cooked
    potatoes, cherry tomatoes, zucchini, canned water chestnuts

Combine curry sauce ingredients in a small pan. Heat until butter melts; stir to blend. Select 3 or more kabob foods and thread on skewers. Under broiler or above hot charcoal, turn and brown each side of kabob, 2 to 3 minutes, basting with curry sauce. Brush food again with sauce before serving.

SKILLET CHOPS WITH RICE

Yield: 4–6 servings

    4–6 thick pork, lamb, or veal chops
    salt and pepper
    2 tablespoons vegetable oil
    1 small onion, chopped
    ½ cup sliced celery
    1¼ cups water
    3 tablespoons honey
    1 teaspoon salt
    ½ teaspoon crumbled sweet basil
    2 cans (8 ounces each) or 1 can (15 ounces) tomato sauce with
        tomato bits
    1 cup regular or converted uncooked white rice
    1 package (10 ounces) frozen peas

Sprinkle chops with salt and pepper; brown well on both sides in an oiled skillet. Remove chops; sauté onion and celery in the same skillet until soft but not brown. Add water, honey, salt, basil, and tomato sauce; bring to a boil. Stir in rice and frozen peas. Place chops in rice mixture, cover tightly, and simmer 30 to 35 minutes.

Whenever it is necessary to broadcast the location of the bee colony to all its members, bees at the entrance will hold their abdomens high and move their wings to fan the scent. This is known as "scenting."

ALL-AMERICAN BARBEQUE BASTING SAUCE

Yield: 7 cups

3 teaspoons chili powder
3 teaspoons black pepper
3 teaspoons dry mustard
3 teaspoons paprika
9 tablespoons honey
6 teaspoons salt
4¹/₂ cups beer
1¹/₂ cups vinegar
12 tablespoons bacon drippings
3 tablespoons Worcestershire sauce
3 tablespoons hot red pepper sauce
4¹/₂ tablespoons lemon juice
4¹/₂ tablespoons grated onions
6 cloves garlic or 6 teaspoons garlic powder

Combine ingredients; simmer 20 minutes over low heat. Refrigerate up to 6 months, using as needed. This sauce is delicious with chicken. The recipe will baste 5 slabs of ribs.

BARBEQUE SAUCE

Yield: 3 cups

¹/₂ cup chopped onion
2 garlic cloves
1¹/₂ cups ketchup
2 tablespoons vinegar
¹/₂ teaspoon salt
1 teaspoon prepared mustard
¹/₂ teaspoon black pepper
2 tablespoons thick commercial steak sauce
1 cup honey

Mix ingredients and cook over low heat for 5 to 7 minutes. Use to baste beef, pork, or chicken.

SPICY BARBEQUE SAUCE

Yield: 2 cups

$^1/_2$ cup honey
$^3/_4$ cup soy sauce
$^3/_4$ cup lemon juice
1 teaspoon dry mustard
1 teaspoon ground ginger
$^1/_8$ teaspoon ground cloves
2 tablespoons commercial steak sauce

Combine ingredients in a small saucepan. Bring to a boil and remove from heat. Use to baste meat.

BEE DREAM

If I could only be a bee,
The flowers would nod and talk with me,
And I would understand the words
They speak to butterflies and birds.
My wings would fan the air so fast,
You'd hear a hum when I went past,
And I would see a world of things
Unknown to dictators and kings.
Wherever I might chance to roam,
The flowers all would be at home
With welcome on their pretty faces
For one with news from distant places.
If I could only be a bee,
I would not care to go to sea.
I'd be a pirate of the land
Who'd gather pollen gold like sand.
I'd cruise about beneath the sky
In which the June clouds drifted high.
Free as the merry sun above,
I'd laugh through life and laugh with love.
I'd fill my honey sac and strive
To be the first back to the hive.
I'd seal my load of gold away
To use some bitter winter's day.
But, then at night, when all the stars
Like headlights on a million cars,
Gleamed high above the dewy grass,
I'd count the cooling hours pass
And wish that I was home in bed,
A pillow soft beneath my head,
Hearing my mother say to me
"Why do you wish to be a bee?"

—Anonymous

Desserts

HONEY CUSTARD

Yield: 4 servings

2 eggs
¼ cup honey
¼ teaspoon salt
2 cups milk, scalded
grating of nutmeg

Beat eggs lightly. Add honey, salt, and milk. Blend well. Pour into custard cups. Sprinkle nutmeg on top. Set cups in pan of warm water and bake at 350 degrees for about 50 minutes, or until tip of silver knife inserted into custard comes out clean.

The queen in the hive can always be found by looking for an area where the worker bees are facing each other. In the middle of this court will be the queen.

HONEY LEMON CUSTARD

Yield: 4 servings

2 egg yolks
1 tablespoon honey
grated peel of ½ lemon
2 egg whites
pinch of salt
2–3 drops vanilla extract

Beat egg yolks and honey together. Add lemon. Beat egg whites until stiff; add salt. Fold beaten egg whites into honey custard mixture. Add vanilla. Chill.

> *It has been said that it is hard to find a beekeeper with kidney trouble, bad eyesight, a bad complexion, lameness, cancer, or paralysis.*

CREAMY HONEY MOLD

Yield: 6–8 servings

2 cups milk
2 eggs
1 envelope (1 tablespoon) unflavored gelatin
½ cup honey
¼ cup chopped preserved or candied ginger
1 teaspoon vanilla extract
1 cup heavy cream, whipped

Combine milk and eggs in a heavy saucepan; beat well. Sprinkle gelatin over milk mixture and let it soften; stir in the honey. Cook over low heat until creamy and slightly thickened, stirring constantly. Add ginger and vanilla. Remove from heat. Continue stirring and cool until mixture mounds. Fold in whipped cream. Pour into a 5-cup mold and chill until firm, overnight or several hours. Serve with fresh or frozen peaches or raspberries.

The Bees flew buzzing through the liquid air,
And pitcht upon the top o' th' laurel tree;
When the Soothsayers saw this sight full rare,
They did foretell th' approach of th' enemie.

—Virgil, Aeneid

HONEY MOUSSE

Yield: 6 servings

3 egg yolks
³/₄ cup honey
1 cup heavy cream, whipped
2 egg whites, stiffly beaten

Beat together egg yolks and honey until light. Fold in whipped cream first, and then beaten egg whites. Pack into 1¹/₂-quart mold and freeze.

FRUITED HONEY RING

Yield: 6 servings

1 package (3 ounces) lemon-flavored gelatin
1 cup boiling water
2 medium-sized ripe bananas
¹/₂ cup honey
2 tablespoons lemon juice
²/₃ cup evaporated milk, chilled

Dissolve gelatin in boiling water. Cool. Mash bananas in large bowl or mixer, using medium speed. Blend in honey, lemon juice, and cooled gelatin. Chill until thick but not set. Whip at low speed, gradually adding chilled evaporated milk. Turn mixer to high speed and continue to whip until mixture doubles in volume and thickens. Pour into a lightly oiled 5-cup ring mold. Chill until set.

IT'S-THE-BERRIES DESSERT

Yield: 8 servings

1 package (8 ounces) cream cheese
¼ cup honey
1 package (10 ounces) frozen strawberries, partially thawed
2 cups colored or white miniature marshmallows
1 cup sliced ripe bananas
1 cup whipping cream

Cream together cheese and honey. Fold in strawberries, marshmallows, and bananas. Whip cream until stiff enough to hold its shape; fold into fruit mixture. Spoon into a 1½-quart mold. Refrigerate until firm, about 6 hours or overnight. To unmold, use a spatula to loosen edges and invert over a serving plate. This dessert is soft-textured. (Party or picnic idea: Spoon mixture into eight 6-ounce paper cups. Insert a wooden stick in the center of each. Freeze 30 minutes, then refrigerate several hours or until firm.)

Honeybee, n., any of a certain social honey-producing bees of **Apis** *and related genera: esp: a native European bee of the world (**Apis mellifera**) that is kept for its honey and wax in most parts of the world, has developed into several races differing in size, color, disposition, and productivity, and has escaped to the wild whenever suitable conditions prevail.*

—**Webster's Third New International Dictionary**

PEACHES DIANE

Yield:. 6–8 servings

1/2 cup mild-flavored honey
1 jar (12 ounces) peach or apricot jelly
1/4 cup fresh orange juice, Cointreau, or triple sec
6–8 freestone peaches, sliced and peeled
1 quart vanilla or pistachio ice cream

In a small saucepan, combine honey with jelly. Heat, stirring constantly, until jelly is melted. Add orange juice or liqueur. Cool; then pour over sliced peaches and chill thoroughly. Spoon sauce over scoops of ice cream.

Variations: Substitute strawberry or currant jelly and hulled whole or halved strawberries for peaches.

> *Honey is 99 percent naturally predigested as it comes,*
> *putting little or no strain on the digestive system.*

HONEY BROILED GRAPEFRUIT

Yield: 6 servings

3 grapefruit
12 tablespoons honey

Wash and cut each grapefruit into halves. Loosen pulp from peel with a sharp knife. Remove seeds and cut out tough fibrous center with scissors. Pour 2 tablespoons honey on each half and place on cold broiler rack set about 4 inches below unit. Broil 15 minutes or until slightly brown. Serve at once.

> *Montezuma, the Aztec emperor of Mexico, was paid a*
> *tribute of 700 jars of honey by conquered tribes.*

APPLESAUCE

Yield: 6 servings

6 tart apples
$\frac{1}{2}$ cup honey
$\frac{1}{2}$ cup water
1 slice lemon
6 whole cloves

Wash, peel, and quarter apples. Place honey, water, lemon, and cloves in a saucepan. Cook for 3 minutes. Add apples. Cook until tender. Remove cloves and lemon.

HONEY BAKED APPLES

Yield: 4 servings

4 apples
$\frac{1}{4}$ cup lemon juice
$\frac{1}{2}$ cup honey
1 teaspoon cinnamon
1 tablespoon butter

Pare, core, and quarter apples and place in a baking dish. Pour the lemon juice and honey over apples. Sprinkle with cinnamon and dot with butter. Bake at 350 degrees until apples are tender, 30–45 minutes.

A beekeeper can collect up to 100 pounds of honey per colony per year.

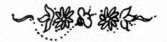

The honeybee is the most widely used and most easily managed insect for pollination. About 80 percent of the insect pollination of crops in the United States is done by honeybees. The remaining 20 percent comes mainly from bumblebees, alfalfa leafcutter bees, and alkali bees.

HONEY STUFFED APPLES

Yield: 6 servings

6 medium-sized cooking apples
$1^1/_3$ cups honey
$^1/_2$ cup water
$^1/_3$ cup Red Hots cinnamon candies or $^1/_4$ teaspoon ground cinnamon
$^2/_3$ cup raisins
$^1/_2$ cup ground coconut

Peel and core apples. In a 10-inch skillet or large saucepan, blend together honey, water, and Red Hots or cinnamon. Bring to a boil; boil 10 minutes or until Red Hots have dissolved. Add apples and cook until fork-tender, but not soft, turning and basting often to cook evenly. Place apples on serving platter or individual dishes. Plump raisins by soaking in a cup of hot water; drain after 5 minutes. Mix raisins and coconut and spoon into centers of apples. Pour cooking syrup over apples. Serve with cream or ice cream.

One level teaspoon of honey weighs approximately 1 ounce. One cup of honey weighs 12 ounces. One pound of honey measures $1^1/_3$ cups.

HONEY BAKED PEARS

Yield: 8 servings

8 pear halves
$\frac{1}{4}$ cup lemon juice
$\frac{1}{2}$ cup honey
1 teaspoon ground cinnamon
2 tablespoons butter

Arrange the pears in a shallow buttered baking pan. Pour the lemon juice and honey over them. Sprinkle with cinnamon and dot with butter. Bake at 350 degrees until done. Serve hot with cream or ice cream.

HONEY CRAN-APPLES

Yield: 8–10 servings

6 medium-sized apples
$\frac{1}{2}$ pound ($2\frac{1}{4}$ cups) cranberries
$1\frac{1}{4}$ cups water
2 cups honey
$\frac{1}{4}$ teaspoon salt
2 cinnamon sticks

Peel and core apples and place in a flat-bottomed pan. Add cranberries and water and simmer 5 minutes, turning apples once during cooking period (turn carefully so apples will be evenly red). Add remaining ingredients. Simmer 15–20 minutes longer or until apples are tender. Remove apples to serving dish, skim the cranberry sauce, and pour sauce around apples. Cool. Cover tightly.

> *The honeybee has been creating its delicious
> and healthful product since long before
> human civilization began.*

HONEY DATE PUDDING

Yield: 12 servings

$1/4$ cup butter
1 cup honey
2 eggs
$1/2$ teaspoon vanilla extract
$2^1/2$ cups whole wheat flour
$2^1/2$ teaspoons baking powder
$1/2$ teaspoon ground cinnamon
$1/2$ teaspoon ground cloves
$1/2$ teaspoon ground nutmeg
$1/2$ teaspoon salt
$3/4$ cup chopped dates
$1/2$ cup chopped pecans
1 cup evaporated milk

Cream butter until light and fluffy. Add honey, eggs, and vanilla; beat 1 minute. In another bowl, sift together flour, baking powder, cinnamon, cloves, nutmeg, and salt; add dates and nuts and mix until dates are flour-coated. Add milk to flour mixture; stir until well blended. Combine two mixtures; pour into a buttered 5-cup mold. Cover tightly with a lid that fits the mold or with foil tied with strong cord. Place in a pressure cooker on a rack. Pour in hot water until it reaches halfway up the side of the mold. Close the cooker lid tightly; start cooker on high heat. Let steam escape for 30 minutes. Place pressure regulator on vent pipe; when regulator begins to rock gently, cook for an additional 45 minutes at medium heat. Remove; cool immediately with cool water. When pressure drops, remove regulator. Remove pudding; take off lid or foil. Cool slightly; remove pudding from mold.

Note: If pudding is steamed on a rack in a steamer or large kettle, steam for 2 hours.

The queen may lay 500,000 eggs during her lifetime.

HONEY DELIGHT

Yield: 6–8 servings

1 package lemon- or orange-flavored gelatin
$1/2$ cup boiling water
$1/2$ cup honey
juice of $1/2$ lemon
1 can evaporated milk, chilled and whipped
$1/2$ pound vanilla wafers, crushed

Dissolve gelatin in boiling water. Add honey and lemon juice and mix well. Fold in the evaporated milk that has been chilled and whipped. Pour this mixture into a pan that has been lined with crushed vanilla wafers. Place additional crushed vanilla wafers on top of mixture and put in refrigerator to set. Cut into squares.

JELLIED PLUM PUDDING

Yield: 8 servings

$3/4$ cup prunes
$3/4$ cup seedless raisins
$1 1/2$ cups boiling water
1 package (3 ounces) cherry- or raspberry-flavored gelatin
2 tablespoons sherry, brandy, or lemon juice
$1/4$ cup honey
$1/4$ teaspoon salt
$1/2$ teaspoon ground cinnamon
$1/2$ teaspoon ground cloves
$1/2$ cup coarsely chopped walnuts or pecans
$1/2$ cup glacé fruit, diced

Soak prunes and raisins in boiling water until fruit plumps. Reserve liquid; chop prunes. Set aside prunes and raisins. Dissolve gelatin in reserved hot liquid. Add sherry, honey, salt, cinnamon, and cloves. Blend well and then chill until slightly thickened. Fold in fruits and nuts. Spoon into a 1-quart mold. Chill until firm. Unmold and serve either plain or with honey-sweetened dairy sour cream or whipped cream. Sprinkle with cinnamon or nutmeg if desired.

A queen bee may live as long as five years.

BAKED PINEAPPLE PUDDING

Yield: 6 servings

 1 can (20 ounces) crushed pineapple
 $\frac{1}{2}$ cup milk
 $\frac{1}{2}$ teaspoon salt
 $\frac{1}{2}$ cup butter
 1 cup mild-flavored honey
 3 eggs
 4 cups dry crustless bread cubes

Drain pineapple well, reserving juice for the sauce. Mix together pineapple, milk, and salt. In a medium mixing bowl, cream butter, beat in honey in a fine stream. Beat in eggs one at a time. Stir in pineapple mixture. In a well-buttered 2-quart casserole, fold together bread cubes and pineapple mixture until cubes are completely moistened. Bake at 325 degrees for 1 hour. Serve hot with a sauce made by combining equal parts honey and pineapple juice or with honey-sweetened whipped cream.

Generally speaking, there are five types of honey on the market today: liquid, comb, solid (sometimes called granulated or crystallized), chunk, and cut comb. Here is a brief description of each:

Liquid honey *is free of visible crystals. It is obtained by uncapping the combs and forcing the honey from the cells by centrifugal motion and differs from comb honey only in the absence of the comb. In the United States, most people prefer honey in the liquid form.*

Granulated or solid honey *is crystallized. Honey in this state is partially or wholly solidified or "sugared" and is often referred to as candied, creamed, or spread. It is very popular in Canada with an increasing demand in the United States.*

Comb honey *is honey in the comb as stored by the bees. Usually comb honey is served in its original size or cut into individual portions. This can be done by cutting squares with a knife dipped in boiling water. Chill 30 minutes before serving to prevent loss of honey from the comb. Serve the individual pieces with a cocktail fork or other small fork.*

Cut comb honey *is made of small chunks of sealed comb honey about 4 inches long and $1^1/2$ inches in width, wrapped in cellophane and packed in individual cartons. In the trade these are known as cut comb or honey hunks.*

Chunk honey *is found mostly in the southern United States. The combs are built in shallow extracting frames and are cut in various-sized chunks that will slip into tin pails or glass jars. The spaces between and around the combs are filled with liquid honey.*

STRAWBERRY-HONEY BAVARIAN

Yield: 6 servings

> 1 package (3 ounces) strawberry-flavored gelatin
> 1 cup hot water
> 1 cup evaporated milk
> juice and grated peel of 1 lemon
> ¼ cup honey
> 18 ladyfingers, split
> 1 package (12 ounces) frozen strawberries

Dissolve gelatin in water; chill until partially set. Pour milk into a plastic bowl and place in freezer until thickened, about 2 hours. Remove and whip until stiff; then add lemon juice, peel, and honey. Beat until well blended. Fold into gelatin; chill until set. Just before serving, partially thaw strawberries and arrange 6 ladyfinger halves around the edges of each of 6 sherbet glasses. Spoon chilled gelatin-cream into glasses and top with strawberries.

> *The basic equipment for the beginning beekeeper should cost no more than $60 and should include a hive, frames, a smoker, a hive tool, a veil, gloves, and a feeder.*

FLORIDA FRUIT CUP

Yield: variable

> ½ cup honey
> 1 cup orange juice
> fresh fruit
> shredded coconut

Mix orange juice and honey. Use any fresh fruit (strawberries, peaches, figs, mangoes, or others). Place each kind of fruit in a separate dish and cover it with the honey–orange juice blend. Marinate the fruit until the flavor is absorbed. Drain the fruits and combine them in a fruit cup. Sprinkle with coconut. Serve as is or with plain angel food cake.

The one queen is the only fertile member of the hive.

HONEY RICE PUDDING

Yield: 8 servings

3 eggs
2 cups cooked rice or ²/₃ cup uncooked rice
3 cups milk
³/₄ cup honey
¹/₂ teaspoon ground cinnamon
1 cup seedless raisins

Butter a 2-quart casserole well. Beat eggs in a large mixing bowl until foamy. Add rice, milk, honey, and cinnamon. Mix well. Stir in raisins. Pour into prepared dish. Bake 1 hour, stirring after 35 minutes to distribute rice and raisins evenly. If uncooked rice is used, check for tenderness and extend cooking time if necessary.

It takes 3 ounces of nectar to produce
1 ounce of honey.

CHOCOLATE FONDUE ROYALE

Yield: 6–8 servings

> $^1/_2$ cup evaporated milk or light cream
> 2 cups or 1 package (12 ounces) semisweet chocolate pieces
> $^1/_2$ cup honey
> $^1/_4$ cup butter
> $^1/_4$ teaspoon salt
> 2 tablespoons orange-flavored liqueur or 1 teaspoon grated
> orange peel and 2 teaspoons fresh orange juice
> 1 teaspoon vanilla extract

ASSORTED DIPPERS
> Cling peach slices, pitted dates, fresh or canned pineapple
> chunks, pretzel twists, fresh strawberries, chunks of fresh
> coconut, fresh unpared apple or pear slices, chunks of angel
> food or sponge cake, tiny filled cream puffs, shelled Brazil
> nuts, ladyfingers (separated), pitted prunes, tiny
> marshmallows, fresh orange sections

Combine milk or cream, chocolate pieces, honey, and butter in fondue pot or heavy saucepan. Place over low heat and cook, stirring constantly, until chocolate is melted and the mixture is smooth. Blend in salt, liqueur, and vanilla. Keep mixture warm over low heat of fondue burner. Serve with a choice of dippers.

HONEY ICE CREAM

Yield: 6–8 servings

> 2 cups milk
> $^3/_4$ cup honey
> $^1/_4$ teaspoon salt
> 2 eggs
> 1 cup whipping cream

Scald milk; add honey and salt. Beat eggs. Pour scalded milk into the egg mixture and stir until well blended. Return to top double boiler and cook over hot water for 3 to 4 minutes. Cool. Whip cream and fold into custard mixture. Freeze in refrigerator. Stir once or twice while freezing.

Bees need four basic materials: nectar, pollen, propolis, and water.

HONEYSCOTCH SUNDAE

Yield: 1¹/₂ cups

> 6 tablespoons butter
> 2 teaspoons cornstarch
> 1¹/₃ cups honey
> ¹/₂ cup chopped pecans

In a saucepan, melt butter over low heat; stir in cornstarch. Add honey and cook, stirring constantly, until mixture boils. Add pecans. Serve warm over ice cream.

HOT FUDGE SUNDAE SAUCE

Yield: 1 cup

> ¹/₃ cup plus 1 tablespoon evaporated milk
> 1 small package (6 ounces) chocolate chips
> ¹/₂ cup honey

In a saucepan, heat milk over low heat. Add chips, stirring until melted. Add honey. Pour over ice cream or cake.

A queen bee may have 2,000 sense plates on its two antennae, a worker bee 6,000, and a drone 30,000.

APPLE CRISP

Yield: 6 servings

> 2 cups sliced pared apples
> 1½ teaspoons lemon juice
> ¼ cup honey
> ¼ cup flour
> 2 tablespoons brown sugar
> ⅛ teaspoon salt
> 2 tablespoons butter

Preheat oven to 375 degrees. Place apples in a lightly buttered baking dish. Combine lemon juice and honey; spread over apples. Mix flour, brown sugar, and salt. Cut or work in butter until mixture is crumbly. Cover apples with flour mixture. Bake 30–40 minutes.

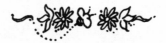

> *A waterproofing for shoes can be made by melting 4 ounces of beeswax and 4 ounces of resin together over gentle heat. Stir in 1 pint of linseed oil. Remove from heat and add ¼ pint of turpentine. When you wish to use this waterproofing, melt the amount needed and rub it well into the leather.*

Cakes

Unless otherwise indicated, each of these recipes will make one cake. The number of servings will vary with the size of the slices.

Unless otherwise specified, use all-purpose flour, double-acting baking powder, and large eggs.

The final step of each recipe is the cooling: cool cakes in pans on a wire rack for 10 minutes. Carefully remove from pan and continue cooling cakes on the racks.

To ensure a tender cake every time, add 2 tablespoons of honey to your favorite cake mix batter.

ELEGANT WHITE FRUIT CAKE

Yield: 2 loaves

1 cup vegetable oil
1½ cups honey
4 eggs
3 cups sifted flour (divided)
1 teaspoon baking powder
¾ teaspoon baking soda
2 teaspoons salt
¾ cup apple juice or pineapple juice
1 pound candied cherries
1 pound pineapple
1 pound dates, pitted and sliced
7–8 cups pecan meats

Grease and line with brown paper two 9-by-5-by-3-inch loaf pans. Preheat oven to 275 degrees. In a mixing bowl, combine oil, honey, and eggs; beat 2 minutes. Sift 2 cups of flour with baking powder, soda, and salt. Stir in oil-honey mixture alternately with juice. Combine fruit and dust thoroughly with remaining cup of flour. Pour batter over fruit, mixing well. Pour batter into prepared pans and bake 2½–3 hours. Cool thoroughly before removing from pans. To store, wrap in foil and keep in a covered container.

HONEY APPLESAUCE CAKE

½ cup shortening
¾ cup honey
2 cups whole wheat flour
¼ teaspoon cloves
½ teaspoon cinnamon
½ teaspoon nutmeg
¼ teaspoon salt
1 teaspoon baking soda
1 cup applesauce
1 cup raisins

Grease an 8-inch square pan. Preheat oven to 350 degrees. Mix shortening and honey well. Stir in dry ingredients, applesauce, and raisins. Bake in prepared pan for 45 minutes.

HONEY-ORANGE-ALMOND CAKE

$^1/_2$ cup shortening
1 cup honey
grated peel of 1 orange
5 egg yolks
2 cups whole wheat flour
2 teaspoons baking powder
$^1/_2$ teaspoon salt
$^1/_2$ cup milk
$^1/_4$ cup ground blanched almonds
slivered almonds

Grease a 9-inch square pan. Preheat oven to 350 degrees. Cream shortening. Add honey gradually, beating until light and fluffy. Add orange peel and mix well. Then add egg yolks, one at a time, beating thoroughly after each addition. Add sifted dry ingredients alternately with milk, beating until smooth. Add ground nuts. Line greased pan with unglazed brown paper, and then grease again. Pour mixture into pan. Bake 50 minutes or until done. Lightly glaze warm cake with honey and decorate with slivered almonds.

Honey has marvelous preservative qualities due to its ability to absorb and retain moisture. It retards drying out and staling of baked goods. If you're baking goodies for children at school, friends a half a continent away, or prebaking party desserts well ahead of time, honey will keep them oven-fresh.

> *Chewing honeycomb provides almost immediate relief
> from allergies such as hay fever.*

SPICED BANANA LAYER CAKE

$1/2$ cup shortening
1 cup honey
2 eggs
2 cups whole wheat flour
2 teaspoons baking powder.
$1/2$ teaspoon baking soda
$1/2$ teaspoon cinnamon
$1/4$ cup honey
$1/4$ cup milk
1 teaspoon vanilla extract
$1/2$ cup mashed ripe banana (1 large or 2 small bananas)

BANANA CREAM FILLING
1 cup whipping cream
2 tablespoons honey
2 ripe bananas, sliced

Prepare cake layers. Grease and flour the bottoms of two 9-inch
round cake pans. Preheat oven to 350 degrees. Cream shortening;
continue creaming while adding 1 cup honey in a fine stream. Add
eggs and beat until well blended. Stir together dry ingredients. Stir
$1/4$ cup honey, milk, and vanilla into mashed banana. Add banana
mixture alternately with dry ingredients to creamed mixture, beginning and ending with dry ingredients. Pour batter into prepared
pans and bake 25–30 minutes until cakes is done. When layers are
cool, either wrap individually to freeze or serve at once. Fill and
frost with banana cream filling just before serving.

To prepare banana cream filling, whip cream until stiff. Sweeten
to taste with honey. Spread half of whipped cream over one layer of
Spiced Banana Layer Cake; cover with half of banana slices. Top

with second layer of cake; frost with whipped cream and garnish with remaining banana slices. (Variations: Place all of the sliced bananas between the layers. Sprinkle the frosted top layer with toasted coconut or flaked, toasted almonds.)

SPICE CAKE

- $1/2$ cup shortening
- 1 cup honey
- 2 cups whole wheat flour
- 2 teaspoons baking powder
- 1 teaspoon salt
- $1/2$ teaspoon ginger
- $1/2$ teaspoon cloves
- $1/2$ teaspoon nutmeg
- 2 eggs, separated
- $3/4$ cup milk
- $1/2$ cup chopped walnuts
- $1/2$ cup raisins

Grease a tube pan. Preheat oven to 350 degrees. Cream shortening; add honey and beat thoroughly. Mix together flour, baking powder, salt, and spices. Add about 1 cup of dry ingredients to shortening and honey mixture. Beat well. Add egg yolks and beat. Add remaining dry ingredients alternately with milk. Add nuts and raisins with last addition of flour. Stir in stiffly beaten egg whites. Pour batter into prepared pan. Bake 60 minutes, or until done.

Enzymes in honey: invertase (converts sucrose to dextrose and levulose), diastase (converts starch to maltose), catalase (decomposes hydrogen peroxide), inulase (converts insulin to levulose), aromatic bodies (terpenes, aldehydes, esters), higher alcohols, maltose, rare sugars

QUICK CINNAMON COFFEE CAKE

2 cups flour
1/2 teaspoon salt
4 teaspoons baking powder
4 tablespoons honey
1 egg, beaten
1 cup milk
4 teaspoons butter or shortening, melted
1/2 teaspoon cinnamon

Grease an 8-inch square pan. Preheat oven to 375 degrees. Sift together flour, salt, and baking powder. Add 2 tablespoons honey, egg, and milk, then melted butter. Stir together. Spread into prepared pan. Dribble remaining honey over top and sprinkle with cinnamon. Bake about 30 minutes. Serve warm. (Suggestion: Press apple slices into top of batter before dribbling honey and cinnamon on.)

> *And as when empty barks on billows float,*
> *With sandy ballast sailors trim the boat,*
> *So bees bear gravel stones whose poising weight*
> *Steers through the whistling winds their steady flight.*
>
> **—Virgil, Georgics**

DUTCH HONEY CAKE

$^1\!/_2$ cup firmly packed dark brown sugar

1 egg

$^1\!/_2$ cup honey

3 tablespoons dark molasses

1 teaspoon baking soda

2 teaspoons water

$^1\!/_2$ teaspoon baking powder

$^1\!/_4$ teaspoon pepper

$^1\!/_4$ teaspoon each of ground allspice, cinnamon, nutmeg,
   and mace

3 tablespoons melted butter

$1^1\!/_2$ cups flour

Grease and flour a 9-by-5-by-3-inch loaf pan. Preheat oven to 350 degrees. Beat together brown sugar and egg. Beat in honey and molasses. Soften baking soda in 2 teaspoons of water and stir into mixture. Combine baking powder, spices, and melted butter. Beat into mixture. Gradually beat in flour a little at a time. Pour mixture into prepared pan. Bake 30–45 minutes, or until a knife blade inserted in the center comes out clean. Cool in pan for 5 minutes; remove and cool on wire rack.

When swarming worker bees find a new location, they literally form a living "curtain," the position in which they begin producing the tiny platelets of wax from the undersides of their abdomens. The platelets become the chambers of the new hive.

HARVEST HONEY CAKE

2 cups whole wheat flour
1 tablespoon baking powder
$^1/_2$ teaspoon baking soda
1 teaspoon salt
1 teaspoon ground cinnamon
1 teaspoon nutmeg
$1^1/_2$ cups finely shredded raw, peeled sweet potatoes
1 cup finely chopped pecans or walnuts
1 cup honey
$^3/_4$ cup vegetable oil
1 teaspoon vanilla extract
4 eggs, separated
$^1/_3$ cup orange juice

Grease and flour a 13-by-9-by-3-inch baking pan or a large bundt pan. Preheat oven to 250 degrees. Combine flour, baking powder, baking soda, salt, cinnamon, and nutmeg. Stir to blend; set aside. Mix shredded sweet potatoes with chopped nuts; set aside. In large bowl of electric mixer, blend together honey, oil, and vanilla. Separate eggs. Beat yolks into honey mixture, one at a time. Fold in potato and nut mixture. Add dry ingredients alternately with orange juice, beating after each addition. Beat egg whites until they hold their shape. Fold thoroughly into cake mixture. Pour into prepared pan. Bake 60 minutes or until cake is done in center. Serve plain or frosted. This cake freezes well.

> *The Hindus claim their god of love had a bow whose string was a chain of bees, symbolizing the sweetness and the sting of love.*

HONEY BUNNY CAKE

$\frac{1}{2}$ cup shortening
$\frac{3}{4}$ cup honey
$\frac{3}{4}$ cup milk
$1\frac{1}{2}$ teaspoons vanilla
$\frac{1}{4}$ teaspoon almond extract
$2\frac{1}{4}$ cups sifted cake flour
$3\frac{1}{4}$ teaspoons baking powder
1 teaspoon salt
$\frac{3}{4}$ cup sugar
4 egg whites
1 recipe Double Boiler Frosting
$1\frac{1}{3}$ cups flaked coconut
jelly beans or gum drops

Grease a 13-by-9-by-2-inch pan and line it with wax paper. Preheat oven to 350 degrees. Cream shortening with honey until well blended. Combine milk, vanilla, and almond extract. Sift dry ingredients and add to shortening and honey. Add $\frac{1}{2}$ cup of the milk and mix until dampened; then beat well. Add egg whites and remaining milk and beat 2 minutes longer. Pour batter into prepared pan and bake 25–30 minutes.

When cake has cooled, cut two strips from corners of one end of cake, each strip $1\frac{1}{2}$ inches wide and 3 inches long. On a large platter, place the large piece of cake; add "ear" strips, slightly slanted.

Prepare Double Boiler Frosting (page 116) and use a little to glue ears to head; spread the rest over the top and sides of the cake. Sprinkle with about 1 cup of coconut. With a drop of red food coloring, tint the remaining coconut pink and spread inside ears. Use jelly beans or gumdrops to form bunny's eyes, nose, and mouth.

HONEY CHOCOLATE CAKE

²/₃ cup shortening
1 cup honey
2 eggs
2 cups whole wheat flour
½ cup cocoa
1 teaspoon salt
½ teaspoon baking soda
2 teaspoons baking powder
¾ cup buttermilk or sour milk
1 teaspoon vanilla

Grease and flour two 9-inch round cake pans. Preheat oven to 350 degrees. Cream shortening; continue beating while slowly adding honey in a fine stream. Beat in eggs, one at a time. Sift together three times: flour, cocoa, salt, soda, and baking powder. Add dry ingredients alternately with the buttermilk or sour milk and vanilla to creamed mixture. Pour batter into prepared pans. Bake 20–25 minutes.

How doth the little busy bee
Improve each shining hour
And gather honey all the day
From every opening flower.

—Isaac Watts

Frostings, Toppings, Sweet Spreads

FLUFFY HONEY FROSTING

Yield: enough for tops and sides of 8-inch layer cake

1 egg white
dash of salt
$^1/_2$ cup honey
$^1/_4$ teaspoon flavoring extract (optional)

Beat egg white with salt until stiff enough to hold up in peaks, but not dry. Pour honey in a fine stream over egg white, beating constantly until frosting holds its shape. If desired, beat in flavoring such as vanilla, lemon, orange, or almond extract.

DOUBLE BOILER FROSTING

Yield: enough for tops and sides of two 9-inch layers

2 egg whites (¼ cup)
¼ teaspoon salt
1 tablespoon water or fruit juice
½ cup honey
½ teaspoon vanilla

In top of double boiler, combine egg whites, salt, and water or juice. Beat until egg whites hold their shape. Continue beating while adding honey in a fine stream. Cook over boiling water, beating constantly, until mixture forms peaks when beater is raised, about 5 minutes. Remove from heat. Add vanilla and beat until frosting is of spreading consistency, about 2 minutes.

Average Chemical Composition of Honey

Principal Components:

Water	17.7%
Levulose (fruit sugar)	40.5%
Dextrose (grape sugar)	34.0%
Sucrose (cane sugar)	1.9%
Dextrins and gums	1.5%
Ash (silica, iron, copper, manganese, chlorine, calcium, potassium, sodium phosphorus, aluminum, sulfur, magnesium)	0.18%
	95.78%

EASY ORANGE FROSTING

Yield: 1 cake topping

$^1/_3$ cup butter
$^1/_2$ cup honey
$^1/_4$ cup frozen orange juice concentrate, unsweetened
1 cup non-instant dry milk powder

Mix together. Beat. Spread. Add chopped nuts if desired.

Foreign bacteria cannot live in raw, uncooked honey.

FLUFFY PEPPERMINT FROSTING

Yield: enough for tops and sides of two 9-inch layers

2 egg whites
$^1/_4$ teaspoon salt
1 tablespoon water
$^1/_2$ cup mild-flavored honey
1 teaspoon vanilla
1 cup crushed peppermint candies
several whole peppermint candies (optional)

In top of double boiler, combine egg whites, salt, and water. With electric mixer, beat until egg whites firm, about 1 minute. Continue beating while slowly adding honey. Cook over boiling water, beating constantly until mixture forms stiff peaks whenever mixer is raised, about 5 to 7 minutes. Remove from heat. Add vanilla and crushed peppermint candy. Beat until frosting is thick enough to spread, about 2 minutes. Decorate frosted cake with whole candies.

LEMON FLUFF FROSTING

Yield: 3 cups

2 egg whites
$1/8$ teaspoon salt
$2^1/2$ cups honey
1 cup powdered sugar
1 tablespoon lemon juice
1 tablespoon grated lemon peel

Beat egg whites and salt until they hold a soft peak. Pour honey in a fine stream over egg whites, beating constantly. Add powdered sugar and lemon juice, alternately. Beat well. Fold in grated lemon peel. Spread on top of cookies.

Like drones and the queen bee, workers have four wings, six hairy legs with hooked feet, sense organs, a sucking tongue, and biting jaws. But only the workers have, in addition, organs for making wax and a special apparatus for collecting nectar and pollen.

HONEY COCONUT TOPPING

Yield: 1 cake topping

3 tablespoons butter
$1/4$ cup evaporated milk or light cream
$1/2$ cup honey
$1/2$ teaspoon vanilla extract
1 cup tightly packed chopped coconut

In a saucepan, combine butter, cream, honey, and vanilla. Bring to a slow boil over low heat, stirring constantly. Remove from heat. Add coconut and blend well. Spread over the top of a warm cake. Broil until coconut is lightly browned. This is good on spice cake.

HONEY CREAM-CHEESE TOPPING

Yield: 1 cup

$^1/_4$ cup honey
1 package (3 ounces) cream cheese, softened
2 tablespoons butter
1 teaspoon vanilla
1 cup dry milk powder

Place honey, cream cheese, butter, and vanilla in a mixing bowl. Beat until fluffy. Add dry milk and beat well. Serve on sliced cake. If desired, garnish with toasted almonds, whole or sliced.

FESTIVE TOPPING

Yield: 2 cups

2 tablespoons butter
$^1/_4$ teaspoon salt
$^1/_3$ cup creamed honey
2 tablespoons evaporated milk or light cream
$^1/_2$ cup diced candied fruit
$^1/_2$ cup slivered almonds
$^1/_2$ cup shredded coconut

In a small bowl, combine butter, salt, honey, and milk. Add fruit, almonds, and coconut; mix well. Spread on cake and place under broiler about 2–4 minutes or until topping is bubbling and almonds lightly brown. Watch carefully to prevent burning.

> *The honeybee forces its way to the base of the flower to obtain nectar for food. In doing this, the bee accidentally rubs pollen on its body and on the stigma.*

ORANGE TOPPING

Yield: 1^1/$_2$ cups

> 2 tablespoons butter, melted
> 3 tablespoons honey
> 2 tablespoons orange juice
> 2 tablespoons lemon juice
> 1^1/$_2$ cups confectioners' sugar

Blend ingredients well.

LEMON SAUCE

Yield: 2^3/$_4$ cups

> 2 tablespoons cornstarch
> 1^3/$_4$ cups water
> ^{3}/$_4$ cup honey
> 1 egg, well beaten
> ^{1}/$_4$ teaspoon salt
> ^{1}/$_4$ cup lemon juice
> 2 teaspoons grated lemon peel

Mix cornstarch with a small amount of water until smooth. Add remaining water, honey, egg, and salt; blend well. Cook and stir until mixture thickens and comes to a boil. Remove from heat; stir in lemon juice and lemon peel.

> *The flavor, color, and composition of honey depend on many factors, including the type of flowers the nectar comes from, the season of the year when it is collected, the weather at the time of collection, and the nature of the soil where the plants grow.*

HONEY BUTTER

Yield: ³/₄ cup

¹/₂ cup butter, softened
¹/₃ cup mild-flavored honey

Blend well and refrigerate. Spread on toast, pancakes, waffles, or plain cakes. (Variations: Add 2 tablespoons orange or lemon juice plus 1 teaspoon of grated peel; or add ¹/₂ cup chopped pitted prunes; or 1 teaspoon cinnamon.)

> *Bees cannot see red, but they can see ultraviolet.*

LEMON-HONEY SPREAD

Yield: 1 quart

2¹/₂ cups honey
grated peel of 1 lemon
³/₄ cup strained lemon juice
¹/₃ cup (¹/₂ bottle) liquid pectin

Combine honey, lemon peel, and lemon juice in a saucepan. Bring to a rolling boil, stirring constantly. Stir in pectin. Bring again to a full boil. Boil for exactly 1 minute. Remove from heat when jelly sheets from a spoon. Skim. Pour into hot, sterilized jelly glasses. Seal with paraffin.

Note: This is delicious on hot toast, pancakes, or waffles, or with cold meats.

Some of the crops that require or are greatly benefited by honeybees for pollination:

alfalfa, almonds, apples, apricots, asparagus, beets, blackberries, blueberries, broad bean, broccoli, brussels sprouts, buckwheat, cabbage, cantaloupe, carrots, cauliflower, celery, cherries, Chinese cabbage, chives, chestnuts, collards, cucumbers, dewberries, field beans, flax, garlic, gooseberries, gourds, grapes, horseradish, huckleberries, kale, kohlrabi, leek, lespedeza, lettuce, lima beans, mustard, okra, onions, parsley, parsnips, peaches, pears, plums, pumpkin, radish, rape, raspberries, red currants, rhubarb, rutabaga, safflower, sainfoin, squash, strawberries, sunflower, trefoil, turnip, vetch, and watermelon

Cookies

Unless otherwise specified, use all-purpose flour, double-acting baking powder, and large eggs.

When a recipe calls for creaming butter, margarine, or shortening with honey, add the honey gradually in a fine stream, beating continuously.

Roll cookies must be chilled several hours to firm the dough before rolling and cutting in shapes.

For ease in removal of cookies, use flat baking sheets with at least one even edge off which cookies may slide. Unless the recipe instructs otherwise, let the baked cookies cool a few minutes before sliding them off the baking sheets onto wire racks for cooling.

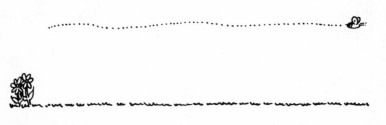

JUST PLAIN HONEY COOKIES

Yield: 72

5–6 cups whole wheat flour
3 eggs
2 cups honey
1 teaspoon ground cinnamon
$^1/_2$ teaspoon salt
3 teaspoons baking soda
1 teaspoon vanilla extract

Reserve 1 cup flour and vanilla; combine remaining ingredients. Let stand in refrigerator overnight. In the morning, add 1 teaspoon vanilla, and enough flour to make a stiff dough. Preheat oven to 350 degrees. Separate dough into big drops and place on greased baking sheets. Bake 12–15 minutes, or until golden brown.

HONEY DROP COOKIES

Yield: 48

$^2/_3$ cup shortening
$1^1/_4$ cups honey
1 egg
$1^1/_2$ teaspoons vanilla extract
$^1/_2$ cup raisins, chopped
$2^1/_2$ cups whole wheat flour
3 teaspoons baking powder
$^1/_4$ teaspoon salt

Grease baking sheets. Preheat oven to 350 degrees. Cream together thoroughly the shortening, honey, and egg. Add vanilla and raisins. Stir together flour, baking powder, and salt; add to creamed mixture and mix just enough to combine the ingredients. Drop by spoonfuls about 2 inches apart on baking sheets. Bake about 14 minutes. Cool on a wire rack.

HONEY GINGER COOKIES

Yield: 72

> 1 cup shortening
> 2 cups honey
> 1 egg, lightly beaten
> 3 cups whole wheat flour
> 2 teaspoons baking powder
> 1 teaspoon ground ginger
> 1 cup chopped nuts

Grease two baking sheets. Preheat oven to 375 degrees. Melt shortening over low heat, then cool. When cool, mix with honey and egg. Sift flour, baking powder, and ginger together and stir in the nuts. Mix dry ingredients with the honey mixture thoroughly and drop by tablespoonfuls onto baking sheets, about 3 inches apart to allow for spreading. Bake 12–15 minutes.

HONEY NUT DROPS

Yield: 48

> 1 cup honey
> 1 cup firmly packed brown sugar
> 1 cup lard or $^1\!/_2$ cup lard and $^1\!/_2$ cup butter
> 1 egg
> $^1\!/_2$ teaspoon salt
> 2 tablespoons ground cinnamon
> $^1\!/_2$ cup chopped nuts
> $3^1\!/_2$ cups flour
> 3 tablespoons baking powder

Cream together honey, brown sugar, lard, and egg; when smooth, add salt, cinnamon, and nuts. Fold in flour gradually, adding baking powder last. Refrigerate at least 1 hour. Grease baking sheets. Preheat oven to 375 degrees. Drop from a teaspoon onto baking sheets and bake 10–12 minutes. (Variations: Add raisins or currants along with the nuts.)

CHEWY NUT COOKIES

Yield: 42

> 2 cups whole wheat flour
> 1 teaspoon salt
> $\frac{1}{2}$ teaspoon baking powder
> $\frac{1}{2}$ teaspoon baking soda
> $\frac{1}{2}$ cup butter or margarine
> 1 cup honey
> $\frac{1}{2}$ cup sour cream
> 2 teaspoons vanilla extract
> 1 cup uncooked quick-cooking oats
> 1 cup broken walnuts
> 2 cups seedless raisins

Stir to combine flour, salt, baking powder, and soda. In a large mixing bowl, cream butter; continue creaming while adding honey in a fine stream. Stir in sour cream and vanilla. Blend in flour mixture and oats. Stir in walnuts and raisins. Chill dough for 30 minutes. Preheat oven to 325 degrees. Drop by tablespoonfuls onto well-greased baking sheets. Bake above oven center for 15 to 20 minutes, or until lightly browned. Cool on wire rack.

> *You should remove the stinger immediately if stung by a bee (without squeezing or pinching if possible), minimizing the amount of venom entering the wound.*

HONEY WHOLE WHEAT CHIPPERS

Yield: 36

$1/2$ cup butter
$1/2$ cup honey
1 egg
$1^{1}/_{4}$ cups whole wheat flour
$1/2$ teaspoon baking soda
$1/2$ teaspoon salt
$1/2$ teaspoon vanilla extract
1 cup chocolate pieces
$1/2$ cup chopped pecans

Grease baking sheets. Preheat oven to 375 degrees. Cream butter and honey together; add egg and beat well. Stir together dry ingredients and add to creamed mixture. Blend well. Add vanilla, chocolate pieces, and pecans; mix well. Drop by rounded teaspoons onto baking sheets. Bake 12–15 minutes. Cool on wire rack.

CHOCOLATE CHIP HONEY COOKIES

Yield: 36

$1/2$ cup butter
$1/2$ cup honey
1 egg
$1/2$ teaspoon vanilla extract
1 cup flour
1 teaspoon baking powder
$1/4$ teaspoon salt
1 cup chocolate chips
1 cup salted peanuts, chopped

Grease baking sheets. Cream butter; continue creaming while adding honey in a fine stream. When mixture is light and fluffy, add the egg and beat well. Add vanilla. Sift flour with baking powder and salt; add to creamed mixture. Fold in chocolate chips and chopped peanuts. Chill dough, and then drop from a teaspoon onto prepared baking sheets while preheating oven to 350 degrees. Bake 12 minutes; cool on wire rack.

> *The Bible mentions a beehive in the chest cavity*
> *of a lion's skeleton.*

HONEY LEMON COOKIES

Yield: 60

$3^{1}/_{2}$ cups whole wheat flour
1 teaspoon baking soda
$^{1}/_{2}$ teaspoon salt
$^{1}/_{2}$ cup butter
$^{1}/_{2}$ cup honey
2 eggs
1 teaspoon grated lemon peel
3 tablespoons lemon juice
1 cup chopped nuts

Grease baking sheets. Preheat oven to 375 degrees. Combine flour, soda, and salt. Cream together butter and honey until light and fluffy. Add eggs and beat well. Add lemon peel and lemon juice; blend well. Add flour mixture and nuts. Mix well. Drop spoonfuls 2 inches apart on baking sheets. Bake about 15 minutes. Cool on a wire rack.

OATMEAL HONEY NUT COOKIES

Yield: 72

$^{3}/_{4}$ cup shortening
$^{3}/_{4}$ cup honey
2 eggs, beaten
$^{1}/_{2}$ cup buttermilk
$^{1}/_{4}$ teaspoon salt
1 teaspoon ground cinnamon
2 cups quick-cooking oats
2 cups flour
1 teaspoon baking soda
$^{1}/_{2}$ cup raisins
$^{1}/_{2}$ cup chopped nuts

Grease baking sheets. Preheat oven to 350 degrees. Cream together shortening and honey. Add remaining ingredients. Drop by tea-spoons onto baking sheets. Bake 12–15 minutes.

WOLVERINE HONEY HERMITS

Yield: 84

$^1\!/_2$ cup shortening
$1^1\!/_2$ cups honey
2 eggs, well beaten
3 tablespoons milk
$2^1\!/_2$ cups whole wheat flour
1 teaspoon baking soda
$^1\!/_2$ teaspoon ground cinnamon
$^1\!/_2$ teaspoon allspice
1 cup seedless raisins
1 cup currants
1 cup dates
$^1\!/_2$ cup nuts

Grease baking sheets. Preheat oven to 400 degrees. Cream shorten-ing, add honey, well-beaten eggs, milk, and remaining ingredients. Drop from a teaspoon onto baking sheets. Bake 10–12 minutes.

A colony, or commune, of bees consists of between 70,000 and 80,000 members. Almost all are female, with a few males (drones) kept around for the sole purpose of propagating the race, and one queen.

HONEY WINE COOKIES
Yield: 60

$^1/_2$ cup shortening
1 cup plus 2 tablespoons honey
2 eggs, separated
$^1/_2$ teaspoon grated lemon peel
$2^3/_4$ cups whole wheat flour
$^3/_4$ teaspoon salt
1 teaspoon baking soda
$^1/_4$ cup white wine
nuts
confectioners' sugar

Grease baking sheets. Preheat oven to 350 degrees. Cream shortening; add honey in a fine stream, beating only to blend. Add egg yolks and lemon peel. Combine dry ingredients; add to creamed mixture alternately with wine. Add nuts. Beat egg whites and fold into batter. Drop by teaspoonfuls onto baking sheets. Bake 12–15 minutes. Dust with confectioners' sugar. Delicious.

HONEY QUEEN KISSES
Yield: 72

1 cup butter
1 cup honey
2 eggs
2 cups whole wheat flour
2 teaspoons baking powder
$^1/_2$ teaspoon salt
1 cup coconut
1 cup butterscotch chips
4 cups corn flakes

Grease baking sheets. Preheat oven to 350 degrees. In a large mixing bowl, cream butter, adding honey a small amount at a time to keep it thick and creamy. Add eggs one at a time, beating well after each addition. Stir together flour, baking powder, and salt in another bowl. Add flour mixture to creamed mixture in thirds, keeping the mixture thick and fine. Add coconut and chips; mix well. Finally, add corn flakes, folding in lightly. Drop by teaspoonfuls onto baking sheets.

> *Bees probably evolved from a wasplike ancestor, contemporaneously with angiosperm plants, toward the end of the Cretaceous period. This beginning of cross-pollination was mutually sustaining to the bees and the plants.*

HONEY APPLESAUCE COOKIES

Yield: 66

3 cups whole wheat flour
3/4 teaspoon baking powder
1 1/4 teaspoons salt
1/2 teaspoon baking soda
1 teaspoon cinnamon
1/4 teaspoon cloves
3/4 cup butter or shortening
1 teaspoon grated lemon peel
1 cup honey
2 eggs
3/4 cup applesauce
3/4 cup coarsely chopped nuts
1 cup raisins

Preheat oven to 400 degrees. Sift flour with baking powder, salt, soda, and spices. Cream butter with lemon peel; add 1/2 cup honey, creaming until light and fluffy. Add eggs and second 1/2 cup of honey; beat well. Then add flour, alternately with applesauce, a small amount at a time, beating after each addition until smooth. Mix in nuts and raisins. Drop by teaspoonfuls onto greased baking sheets, 2 inches apart. Bake about 12 minutes. Cool and store in tightly covered container.

CORN FLAKE DROP COOKIES

Yield: 36

¼ cup butter
1 cup honey
1 egg
½ cup chopped pecans
½ cup shredded coconut
4 cups corn flakes

Grease baking sheets. Preheat oven to 350 degrees. Cream butter; add honey and continue creaming until light and fluffy. Add egg and mix well. Add pecans, coconut, and corn flakes and mix. Drop by spoonfuls onto baking sheets. Bake about 10 minutes. Cool on a wire rack.

Royal jelly—or bee milk—is a special food that the worker bees produce in their nursing glands. All larvae are fed royal jelly at first, but the workers are switched to a mixture of pollen and honey after the first 60 hours. The queen-to-be is fed royal jelly throughout the larval stage.

PEANUT BUTTER HONEY COOKIES

Yield: 72

$^1/_2$ cup shortening
$^1/_2$ cup honey
$^1/_2$ cup firmly packed brown sugar
$^1/_2$ cup chunky peanut butter
1 egg, beaten
2 cups whole wheat flour
$^1/_2$ teaspoon baking powder
$^1/_2$ teaspoon baking soda
$^1/_2$ teaspoon salt

Mix shortening, honey, brown sugar, peanut butter, and egg together, and stir dry ingredients into the peanut butter and honey mixture. Chill dough several hours. Preheat oven to 375 degrees. Roll dough into walnut-size balls and place 3 inches apart on ungreased baking sheets. Flatten and crisscross with a fork dipped in sugar. Bake until set, 10–12 minutes.

HONEY NUT COOKIES

Yield: 48

1 cup butter or margarine
1 cup honey
1 egg
1 teaspoon orange juice
2 cups flour
$^1/_2$ teaspoon salt
1 teaspoon baking soda
1 cup chopped nuts
$^1/_2$ teaspoon baking powder

Grease baking sheets. Preheat oven to 375 degrees. Cream butter. Add honey, egg, and orange juice. Beat well. Sift dry ingredients and add to above mixture. Add $^1/_2$ cup chopped nuts and mix well. Roll teaspoonfuls of mixture in remaining chopped nuts. Place on baking sheets and bake about 12 minutes. Cool on a wire rack.

BUTTER COOKIES

Yield: 96

2 eggs, separated
8 cups whole wheat flour
1¼ teaspoons baking powder
2 cups butter
1 cup honey
grated peel and juice of ½ lemon
1 cup almonds, chopped

Lightly beat egg yolks. Combine flour with baking powder in another bowl. Cream butter with honey; add yolks, flour mixture, lemon peel, and juice. Chill dough until firm. Before shaping cookies, preheat oven to 350 degrees. Either form small balls of dough or roll dough on a floured surface and cut with floured cookie cutters. Place cookies on lightly greased baking sheets. Brush with beaten egg whites and sprinkle with chopped almonds. Bake 10–15 minutes.

These cookies keep well.

> *Guard bees are absolutely fearless, attacking any intruder, including man—who, at 160 pounds, would be 560,000 times their size.*

COCONUT HONEY CRISPS

Yield: 48

2 cups whole wheat flour
1½ teaspoons baking powder
¼ teaspoon salt
¾ cup softened butter or margarine
1 cup firmly packed brown sugar
1 egg
½ cup honey
2 teaspoons vanilla extract
1 cup coconut

Stir together flour, baking powder, and salt. Cream butter; add brown sugar gradually until smooth. Mix in egg, honey, and vanilla. Stir in dry ingredients and coconut until thoroughly combined. Shape into a cylinder or roll, wrap in wax paper, and refrigerate at least 3 hours or overnight. When ready to bake, preheat oven to 375 degrees and slice firm dough about $1/4$ inch thick. Place slices on ungreased baking sheets; press the top of each with floured fork tines. Bake 12–15 minutes. Cool on a wire rack.

HOLIDAY HONEY GINGER COOKIES

Yield: 60

2 cups sifted flour
$1/8$ teaspoon baking soda
$1/3$ cup honey
$1/2$ teaspoon ground ginger
$1/2$ teaspoon salt
$1/2$ cup sugar
2 tablespoons water
1 egg, lightly beaten
1 teaspoon orange extract
$1/2$ cup chopped crystallized ginger
$1/2$ cup chopped blanched almonds

Sift flour once, measure, add soda, and sift again. Place honey, ginger, salt, sugar, water, egg, and orange extract in a bowl and beat with a rotary beater until well blended. Add crystallized ginger and nuts, mixing thoroughly. Stir in flour. Chill thoroughly. When ready to bake, preheat oven to 325 degrees. On a lightly floured surface, roll dough $1/4$ inch thick and cut into shapes. Brush cookies with egg and sprinkle with colored sugar or tiny Christmas candy mixtures. Bake on ungreased baking sheets for 12–15 minutes. Cool on a wire rack. Store in an airtight container.

HONEY ICEBOX COOKIES

Yield: 48

2$\frac{1}{2}$ cups whole wheat flour
2 teaspoons baking powder
$\frac{1}{2}$ teaspoon salt
$\frac{1}{2}$ teaspoon ground cinnamon
$\frac{1}{2}$ cup chopped walnuts
1 egg, well beaten
$\frac{1}{4}$ teaspoon almond extract
1 cup honey
$\frac{3}{4}$ cup melted shortening

Combine sifted flour with baking powder, salt, and cinnamon, and sift again. Add nuts. Combine egg, almond extract, honey, and shortening; add to flour-nut mixture, mixing well. Shape in rolls, 1$\frac{1}{2}$ inches in diameter, and roll each in wax paper. Chill overnight or until firm enough to slice. To bake, preheat oven to 400 degrees. Cut dough rolls in $\frac{1}{8}$-inch slices; place on ungreased baking sheets and bake for 10 minutes. Cool on wire rack.

HONEY CORNUCOPIAS

Yield: 72

$\frac{1}{2}$ cup butter
$\frac{1}{4}$ cup honey
1 egg
1 cup whole wheat flour
$\frac{1}{8}$ teaspoon ground nutmeg
$\frac{1}{4}$ teaspoon ground cinnamon
$\frac{1}{2}$ cup shredded almonds

Grease baking sheets; preheat oven to 350 degrees. Cream butter and honey well. Add egg and beat well. Add flour, spices, and nuts; mix just enough to combine ingredients. Drop from a teaspoon about 6 inches apart onto baking sheets and spread thin. Bake about 8–10 minutes. When done, remove cookies from pan and form into cone shapes while still warm. Fill with chopped dried fruit moistened with honey, cream cheese softened with honey, Honey Coconut Filling (page 146), or your favorite filling.

> *Some people claim that an improved diet, including raw foods and honey, has eliminated tuberculosis.*

HONEY LACE WAFERS

Yield: 36

 $^{1}/_{2}$ cup whole wheat flour
 $^{1}/_{4}$ teaspoon baking powder
 $^{1}/_{8}$ teaspoon baking soda
 $^{1}/_{2}$ cup honey
 $^{1}/_{4}$ cup butter
 $^{1}/_{2}$ cup shredded coconut
 $1^{3}/_{4}$ teaspoons grated orange peel

Grease baking sheets; preheat oven to 350 degrees. Stir flour together with baking powder and soda. Combine honey and butter in a saucepan. Bring to a full boil and cook 1 minute; remove from heat. Add dry ingredients, coconut, and orange peel; mix well. Drop by $^{1}/_{4}$ teaspoonfuls on baking sheets. Bake only 6 at a time for ease in handling cookies. Bake 8–10 minutes. Remove each wafer carefully from baking sheet while still warm and roll quickly over the handle of a wooden spoon. Place on a rack to cool. Serve with compote of orange sections, canned pears, and cherries or your favorite combination of fruits.

In Greek and Roman mythology, honey was considered food for kings and gods. Guests were greeted with fresh honey.

LEBKUCHEN

Yield: 72

4 cups whole wheat flour
$1/4$ teaspoon baking soda
$3/4$ teaspoon ground cinnamon
$1/8$ teaspoon ground cloves
$1/8$ teaspoon ground nutmeg
$2/3$ cup honey
$1/2$ cup firmly packed brown sugar
2 tablespoons water
1 egg, lightly beaten
$3/4$ cup (3 ounces) shredded candied orange peel
$3/4$ cup (3 ounces) shredded candied citron
1 cup blanched and shredded almonds

TRANSPARENT GLAZE
1 cup sifted confectioners' sugar
$1^1/2$ tablespoons boiling water
$1/2$ teaspoon vanilla extract

Combine flour with soda and spices. Combine honey, sugar, and water and boil for 5 minutes. Cool. Add flour mixture, egg, fruits, and nuts. Press dough into a cake, wrap in wax paper, and refrigerate 2–3 days to ripen. When ready to bake, grease baking sheets and preheat oven to 350 degrees. On a floured surface, roll $1/4$-inch-thick strips of dough. Bake 15 minutes; cool on wire racks. When cool, spread with transparent glaze.

Prepare transparent glaze. Combine confectioners' sugar and boiling water. Add vanilla. Beat thoroughly, and then spread on Lebkuchen while glaze is still warm.

Note: Store Lebkuchen 2 weeks or longer for best flavor.

LECKERLI

Yield: 36

$\frac{1}{4}$ cup finely chopped citron
$\frac{1}{4}$ cup finely chopped candied lemon peel
$\frac{1}{4}$ cup finely chopped candied orange peel
$\frac{1}{4}$ cup finely chopped blanched almonds
1 tablespoon cinnamon
1 teaspoon cloves
$1\frac{2}{3}$ cups honey
2 eggs
2 teaspoons baking soda
2 teaspoons hot water
1 tablespoon orange juice
2 cups whole wheat flour

Combine fruits, nuts, spices, and 1 cup honey. Add beaten eggs and mix well. Bring $\frac{2}{3}$ cup honey to the boiling point and cool. Moisten soda in the hot water and add to fruit mixture. Add cooled honey and orange juice. Add flour and stir just enough to combine ingredients. Chill overnight. Roll part of dough at a time, about $\frac{1}{4}$ inch thick (dough will be soft). Cut into rectangular strips $2\frac{1}{2}$ by 1 inch. Place on greased cookie sheet and bake at 350 degrees for about 15 minutes or until done.

Honeybees and wild bees pollinate hundreds of species of wild plants, shrubs, and trees that provide soil cover and produce seeds and berries for birds, insects, and other animals. These ecological relationships are vital to our food supply and to our environment. If they are to continue, we must maintain a beekeeping industry and move toward greater knowledge and more enlightened conservation of our bee resources.

> *Honey is a sweet, viscid, yellow fluid, the nectar*
> *of flowers collected by bees.*
>
> **—Oxford Dictionary**

BROWNIES

Yield: 32

4 tablespoons butter
2 ounces unsweetened chocolate
1 cup honey
⁵⁄₈ cup whole wheat flour
1 teaspoon baking powder
¹⁄₄ teaspoon salt
¹⁄₃ cup chopped nuts

Grease an 8-inch square pan well. Preheat oven to 275 degrees. In top of a double boiler over hot water, melt butter and chocolate, stirring well. Add honey and mix thoroughly. Remove from heat. Combine flour with baking powder and salt; stir into chocolate mixture. Add nuts; stir just enough to combine. Spread in prepared pan and bake about 60 minutes. Cool slightly in pan; then cut in 1-by-2-inch pieces and remove to cooling racks.

> *Some areas of the United States produce unusual honey*
> *products due to certain species of honey plants that are*
> *unique to that particular area: southern Georgia—*
> *gallberry; western Florida—tupelo; California—sages;*
> *west Texas—huajillo and white brush; the Alleghe-*
> *nies—sourwood; Massachusetts—sweet pepperbush; the*
> *Catskills—thyme; northern New York—blue thistle.*

HONEY WALNUT COOKIES

Yield: 30

1/2 cup butter
1/3 cup honey
2 eggs
1 teaspoon grated lemon peel
1 1/4 cups whole wheat flour
1/2 teaspoon baking powder
1/2 teaspoon salt
1/4 teaspoon baking soda
1/2 teaspoon ground nutmeg
1/2 teaspoon ground cinnamon
1/2 cup coarsely chopped walnuts
walnut halves or pieces for garnish (optional)

Cream butter; continue creaming while adding honey in a fine stream. Add eggs and beat until well blended. Stir in lemon peel. Combine flour, baking powder, salt, soda, and spices. Add to the creamed mixture, blending only until well mixed. Stir in chopped walnuts. Chill dough for 1 hour or longer until firm. Grease baking sheets. Preheat oven to 325 degrees. Drop by teaspoonfuls about 2 inches apart onto baking sheets. If desired, lightly press a walnut half into top of each cookie. Bake 10–12 minutes.

In a honeybee's dance language, it can communicate a variety of information, such as the type of blossoms found, the degree of maturity of the blossoms, the number of blossoms available, the distance from the hive, the direction, and the amount of interference that would be encountered in procuring the valuable nectar.

BUTTERSCOTCH BROWNIES

Yield: 20

1½ cups whole wheat flour
1 teaspoon baking powder
½ teaspoon salt
½ cup shortening
½ cup firmly packed brown sugar
½ cup honey
1 egg
1 teaspoon vanilla
½ cup chopped nuts

Grease an 8-inch square pan. Preheat oven to 350 degrees. Mix all ingredients together and spread into prepared pan. Bake 25–30 minutes until a slight imprint shows when touched with a finger; don't overbake. Before cooling, cut into bars.

> *Each fall, the Jewish people celebrate the beginning of the new year, and part of the optimistic hope for the future is symbolized by a jar of honey. Honey, one of the symbols of the Jewish New Year, Rosh Hashana, is used during holiday meals as a dip for bread or apple. It signifies hope and sweetness for the coming year.*

HONEY DATE BARS

Yield: 48

$^1\!/_2$ cup shortening
1 cup honey
1 teaspoon vanilla
3 eggs or 6 egg yolks
1$^1\!/_4$ cups whole wheat flour
1 teaspoon baking powder
$^1\!/_2$ teaspoon salt
1 cup chopped dates
1 cup chopped nuts
confectioners' sugar

Grease a 9-by-12-inch pan. Preheat oven to 350 degrees. Blend shortening, honey, and vanilla until creamy. Beat in eggs one at a time. Combine dry ingredients and blend into egg mixture. Add dates and nuts and stir just enough to distribute evenly. Spread in prepared pan. Bake 30–35 minutes. Cool, cut into bars, and roll in confectioners' sugar.

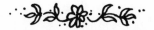

> *Christianity brought with it an increase in honey production due to the increased demand for wax for church candles.*

Pies and Pastries

APPLE-NUT PIE

Yield: 6–8 servings

3 tablespoons whole wheat flour
1/4 teaspoon salt
1 teaspoon ground cinnamon
1/2 teaspoon ground nutmeg
1/2 cup sour cream
3/4 cup honey
1/2 cup chopped pecans
6 medium-sized tart apples
unbaked pastry for 9-inch double-crust pie

Preheat oven to 425 degrees. Mix flour, salt, cinnamon, and nutmeg; add sour cream, honey, and pecans. Peel and slice apples and stir into flour mixture. Line pie pan with half of pastry. Add filling and adjust top crust. Bake 30 minutes; reduce heat to 350 degrees and bake about 15 minutes longer, until crust is golden.

HONEYBEE DIAMONDS

Yield: 24

³/₄ cup butter
³/₄ cup honey
3 eggs
1 cup whole wheat flour
1¹/₂ teaspoons baking powder
¹/₄ teaspoon salt
¹/₂ teaspoon ground cinnamon
¹/₄ cup milk
1 teaspoon grated orange peel
1 cup walnuts, chopped

SYRUP
1 cup honey
¹/₄ cup water
1 tablespoon lemon juice

Grease and flour a 9-by-13-inch pan. Preheat oven to 350 degrees. Cream butter and ³/₄ cup honey; add eggs, one at a time, beating well after each. Stir together flour, baking powder, salt, and cinnamon; add to batter. Stir in milk and orange peel. Beat well and blend in nuts. Pour into prepared pan. Bake 30 minutes or until done. Cool in pan. For syrup, simmer 1 cup honey and water for 5 minutes. Skim and add lemon juice; simmer 2 additional minutes. Cool. Pour syrup over baked pastry; refrigerate. Cut into diamonds to serve.

> *When a honeycomb has been filled with honey*
> *for storage, workers close it with a wax seal*
> *just as a canner seals a jar of preserves.*

HONEY COCONUT FILLING

Yield: enough to fill 36–48 cookie sandwiches (about 2 cups)

1/2 cup water
1 cup honey
3 cups shredded coconut
dash of salt
1/2 teaspoon cornstarch
1 tablespoon butter
1/2 teaspoon vanilla extract

In a saucepan, combine water, honey, coconut, salt, and cornstarch. Cook over low heat for 10 minutes, stirring occasionally. Add butter and vanilla; blend. Cool. Spread between thin cookies, wafers, or honey graham crackers, or use to fill Honey Cornucopias (page 136).

> *Coloration of the white pupa starts with the eyes, which turn pink, then purple, then black-brown. The color then works back toward the rear. The bee is about 14 days old when it begins to take on color.*

DATE NUT COOKIE FILLING

Yield: 1 1/2 cups

1 cup pitted dates, cut in small pieces
1/2 cup honey
1/2 cup water
1/2 cup nuts, finely cut

Cook dates, honey, and water until dates are soft. Add nuts and cool. Excellent with Honey Date Bars (page 143) or Honey Cornucopias (page 136).

> *Six teaspoons of honey spaced throughout the day act as a harmless sedative.*

FIG COOKIE FILLING

Yield: 1¹/₄ cups

¹/₂ cup chopped figs
¹/₂ cup honey
¹/₄ cup water
2 tablespoons orange juice
1 tablespoon cornstarch

Mix ingredients in top of a double boiler and cook over hot water until thick enough to spread.

APPLE-PEAR PIE

Yield: 6–8 servings

3 cups thinly sliced, pared ripe pears (about 3 large pears)
3 cups thinly sliced, pared tart cooking apples (about 4 medium-sized apples)
2 tablespoons lemon juice
1 cup mild-flavored honey
¹/₈ teaspoon salt
¹/₄ cup cornstarch
¹/₂ teaspoon ground nutmeg
unbaked pastry for 9-inch double-crust pie
2 tablespoons butter or margarine

In a large bowl, combine pears and apples; sprinkle with lemon juice and fold in honey. In a small bowl, combine salt, cornstarch, and nutmeg; add to fruit, tossing lightly to combine. Preheat oven to 425 degrees. Line a 9-inch pie plate with half of pastry. Mound fruit mixture over pastry; dot with butter. On a floured surface, roll out remaining pastry to form an 11-inch circle. Cut dough in half-inch strips; arrange half the strips across the pie filling, 1 inch apart. Arrange the remaining strips in the opposite direction to form a lattice. Bind the ends of the strips into the bottom crust as you flute the edge. Bake 50–60 minutes, or until fruit is tender and crust is golden brown. Cool partially on a wire rack; serve while still warm.

MELTS-IN-YOUR-MOUTH BLUEBERRY COBBLER

Yield: 6–8 servings

$1/2$ cup whole wheat flour
$1/4$ cup ground walnuts
$1/2$ cup honey
$1/8$ teaspoon salt
$1/4$ teaspoon ground cinnamon
2 teaspoons lemon juice
1 quart blueberries
unbaked pastry for 9-inch double-crust pie
2 tablespoons butter

Preheat oven to 450 degrees. Combine flour, walnuts, honey, salt, cinnamon, and lemon juice. Slowly fold in blueberries. Pour fruit mixture into pie shell and dot with butter. Top with upper pastry, slicing steam vents in top. Bake for 10 minutes; then turn oven to 350 degrees and bake about 35 minutes or until crust is golden brown.

> *A worker (female) bee is about $1/4$ inch in height, $1/2$ to $5/8$ inches long. It takes about 4,500 workers to weigh 1 pound.*

CHERRY PIE

Yield: 6–8 servings

1 can (21 ounces) pie cherries
$1/4$ teaspoon salt
3 tablespoons cornstarch
$3/4$ cup honey
1 tablespoon butter
$1/8$–$1/4$ teaspoon almond extract
unbaked pastry for 8-inch double-crust pie

Drain cherries, reserving juice, and set aside. Combine juice with salt and cornstarch. Add honey and cook over medium heat, stirring constantly, until thickened and clear. Add butter and stir until melted. Remove from heat and gently stir in cherries and almond extract. Set aside to cool while preparing crust. Preheat oven to 425 degrees. Line an 8-inch pie plate with pastry; spoon in cooled filling. Top with lattice strips of pastry, sealing and fluting edges. Bake 30–35 minutes or until filling is bubbly and crust is lightly browned.

Amor, the god of love, dipped his arrows in honey.

STRAWBERRY PIE

Yield: 8 servings

2 packages (3 ounces each) cream cheese
2 tablespoons honey
dash of salt
$\frac{1}{2}$ teaspoon milk, or more as needed
baked and cooled 9-inch pie shell
$\frac{1}{2}$ cup honey
$\frac{1}{3}$ cup water
1 envelope (1 tablespoon) unflavored gelatin
1 cup crushed strawberries, undrained
2–3 drops red food coloring
$1\frac{1}{2}$–2 cups whole strawberries, hulled and sliced in half

Cream together cheese, honey, and salt; moisten with milk. Spread in pie shell; refrigerate. In a saucepan, combine honey, water, gelatin, crushed berries, and food coloring. Stir over medium heat until slightly thickened and clear, 10–15 minutes. Refrigerate until mixture mounds when stirred. Arrange sliced berries over cream cheese mixture in pie shell; spoon gelatin mixture over all. Chill several hours. (If desired, reserve a few whole or sliced berries as garnish.)

RHUBARB AND RASPBERRY PIE

Yield: 6–8 servings

1 pound (about 4 cups) unpeeled rhubarb
1 cup mild-flavored honey
1 package (3 ounces) raspberry gelatin
2 tablespoons cornstarch
1 egg, lightly beaten
unbaked pastry for 8-inch double-crust pie
2 tablespoons butter

Preheat oven to 425 degrees. Wash and trim rhubarb, but do not peel; cut in $\frac{1}{2}$-inch slices. In a mixing bowl, combine rhubarb with honey, gelatin, cornstarch, and egg. Spread over pastry shell in an 8-inch pie plate and dot with butter. Place top crust over filling, seal edges, and cut a few slits in the top for steam to escape. Bake 35 minutes. Pastry will be brown.

LEMON-HONEY CHIFFON PIE

Yield: 6–8 servings

1 envelope (1 tablespoon) unflavored gelatin
$\frac{1}{4}$ cup cold water
4 eggs, separated
$\frac{3}{4}$ cup honey
$\frac{3}{4}$ teaspoon salt
1 teaspoon grated lemon peel
$\frac{1}{2}$ cup lemon juice
baked and cooled 9-inch pie shell
$\frac{1}{2}$ cup whipped cream or whipped topping (optional)

Soften gelatin in water. In the top of a double boiler, beat egg yolks and combine with honey, salt, lemon peel, and juice. Cook over hot water, stirring, until mixture starts to thicken. Remove from heat, add gelatin, and stir to dissolve. Cool, stirring occasionally. Beat egg whites until stiff; fold into cooled lemon mixture. Pour gently into pie shell. Chill 2 to 3 hours or until firm. Top with whipped cream or topping, if desired.

GRANDMA'S RAISIN PIE

Yield: 6–8 servings

unbaked pastry for 8-inch double-crust pie
3 cups (about 1 pound) raisins
boiling water
$^1/_2$ cup honey
1 tablespoon grated lemon peel
2 tablespoons cornstarch
$^1/_2$ cup cold water

Line an 8-inch pie plate with half of pastry. Chill. In a saucepan, combine raisins and boiling water; stir and bring to a full boil. Mix in honey and lemon peel. Set aside while blending cornstarch and cold water to make a smooth paste. Blend into raisin mixture. Cook and stir until thickened. Preheat oven to 425 degrees. Pour filling into pastry shell. Top with remaining pastry, making several slits near the center for steam vents. Fold edge of top crust under bottom crust; press edges together. Bake 30–45 minutes or until crust is browned.

The only times a queen bee will leave its hive are initiation flights, mating flights, and swarming time.

HONEYCOMB PIE

Yield: 6–8 servings

PASTRY

1 cup sifted flour
$^{1}/_{8}$ teaspoon grated lemon
  peel
$^{1}/_{2}$ teaspoon salt
$^{1}/_{4}$ teaspoon sugar
$^{1}/_{4}$ cup shortening
2 tablespoons butter
2–3 tablespoons cold water

FILLING

$^{3}/_{4}$ cup sifted flour
$^{1}/_{4}$ teaspoon salt
1 teaspoon baking soda
1 cup sugar
3 eggs
$^{1}/_{2}$ cup butter, melted
$^{1}/_{3}$ cup milk
$^{1}/_{4}$ cup lemon juice
$^{1}/_{2}$ teaspoon grated lemon
  peel
1 cup honey

In a mixing bowl, toss together flour, lemon peel, salt, and sugar. Cut in shortening and butter with a pastry blender or blending fork until pieces are the size of rice kernels. Sprinkle water evenly over the mixture and toss with a fork until evenly dampened. On a floured surface, roll out dough to a 10-inch circle. Line a 9-inch pie plate with pastry; flute edge. Chill while preparing filling.

Prepare filling: Sift together flour, salt, and baking soda. Add sugar; toss together lightly. Beat eggs until thick and lemon-colored. Beat in butter, milk, lemon juice, lemon peel, and honey. Stir in dry ingredients and blend well. Pour into chilled unbaked pie shell. Bake at 325 degrees 55–60 minutes. Chill before serving. Top with whipped cream.

CHRISTMAS PIE

Yield: 6–8 servings

4 tablespoons cornstarch
³/₄ cup honey
2 cups boiling water
3 egg whites, stiffly beaten
1 teaspoon vanilla extract
¹/₂ teaspoon almond extract
1 cup whipping cream, whipped
coconut, cherries, or nuts for garnish

In a saucepan, gently cook cornstarch, honey, and water, stirring until well mixed and dissolved. Pour hot mixture over egg whites. Continue beating until stiff, about 10 minutes; stir in extracts. Pour into baked pie shell. Cover with whipped cream. Garnish as desired. Chill for several hours or overnight before serving.

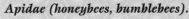

The bee fauna is quite large, possibly 15,000 to 20,000 species and subspecies in North America, north of Mexico. Bees are divided into nine families: Colletidae, Megachilidae (leafcutters), Halictidae, Dasypodaidae, Meganomiidae, Stenotritidae, Andrenidae, Melittidae, Apidae (honeybees, bumblebees).

DOUBLE-DECKER PUMPKIN PIE

Yield: 8 servings

1³/₄ cups canned pumpkin
¹/₂ teaspoon salt
¹/₂ teaspoon ground nutmeg
¹/₂ teaspoon ground ginger
1 teaspoon ground cinnamon
1 cup honey
1 envelope (1 tablespoon) unflavored gelatin
1 cup whipping cream
vanilla ice cream, softened
1 baked 9-inch pastry shell or cookie crust, cooled
¹/₄ cup toasted blanched slivered almonds (optional)

In a saucepan over low heat, gently stir pumpkin, salt, spices, honey, and gelatin about 5 minutes until gelatin is dissolved. Chill until slightly thickened. Whip cream until stiff; combine cooled pumpkin and whipped cream. Spread vanilla ice cream over pastry shell. Top ice cream with pumpkin pie mixture; arrange toasted slivered almonds over top. Place pie unwrapped in freezer. When solidly frozen, about 2 hours, wrap and return to freezer. Remove from freezer about 5 minutes before serving.

Most schoolchildren have been contestants in spelling bees. These single-elimination bees are held on local, state, and national levels.

PILGRIM PUMPKIN PIE

Yield: 6–8 servings

2 eggs
1 can (16 ounces) pumpkin or 2 cups mashed cooked pumpkin
³/₄ cup honey
¹/₂ teaspoon salt
1 teaspoon ground cinnamon
¹/₂ teaspoon ground ginger
¹/₈ teaspoon ground cloves
1²/₃ cups milk or light cream or 1 can (13 ounces)
    evaporated milk
unbaked 9-inch pie shell

In a bowl, beat eggs lightly; then mix in remaining ingredients except pie shell. Pour mixture into pie shell and bake at 425 degrees for 15 minutes. Reduce oven temperature to 350 degrees and bake 45 minutes or until pie is set (knife inserted in center comes out clean).

RHUBARB PIE

Yield: 6–8 servings

1 egg
3¹/₂ cups chopped rhubarb
1 tablespoon flour
1 tablespoon cornstarch
1¹/₄ cups honey
unbaked 9-inch pie shell

Beat egg. Add to chopped rhubarb. Mix flour, cornstarch, and honey in a bowl; add to rhubarb and mix. Pour into pie shell. Bake at 350 degrees for about 45 minutes.

> *Honeybees have two stomachs—one to digest and utilize their own food and a second, social stomach designed especially to transport nectar and honey.*

HONEY CHEESECAKE

CRUMB BASE
2 cups graham cracker
   crumbs
1/2 cup butter, melted
1 teaspoon cinnamon
1/3 cup honey

FILLING
3 tablespoons butter
2 cups cottage cheese, sieved
2 tablespoons sifted flour
1 teaspoon salt
1/3 cup honey
3 tablespoons lemon juice
1 teaspoon grated lemon peel
4 eggs, separated
1/3 cup sugar
2/3 cup milk

Lightly butter the bottom and sides of an 11 1/2-by-7 1/2-inch pan. Stir together crumb base ingredients, reserving 1/2 cup. Press mixture against bottom and sides of prepared pan. Refrigerate crumb base and preheat oven to 350 degrees while preparing the filling. Cream butter, and then blend in cheese, flour, and salt. Beat in honey, lemon juice, and lemon peel. Add egg yolks one at a time, beating well after each addition. Beat whites until stiff; slowly add sugar and beat until soft peaks form. Fold whites into cheese mixture. Gently blend in milk, then pour filling into crumb base. Sprinkle reserved crumb base mix over top. Bake 1 hour; chill before serving.

Delegated jobs in the bee colony include queen's attendants, nurses, housekeepers, water carriers, food gatherers, cradle makers for the young, food storers, undertakers, material gatherers, surveyors, and guards.

CHEESECAKE PIE

Yield: 6–8 servings

CRUST

3/4 cup graham cracker
   crumbs
1/4 cup honey
1/4 cup melted butter or
   shortening

TOPPING

1 tablespoon sugar
1 cup sour cream
1/2 teaspoon vanilla
1/4 cup graham cracker
   crumbs

FILLING

1 package (8 ounces) cream
   cheese
1 cup small-curd creamed
   cottage cheese
1/2 cup honey
2 eggs
2 tablespoons flour
1/2 tablespoon salt
1 tablespoon grated lemon
   peel
1 tablespoon lemon juice
1 teaspoon vanilla extract
dash of ground nutmeg

Prepare crust: Combine ingredients and press against bottom and sides of a well-buttered 9-inch pie plate. Refrigerate for at least an hour.

Prepare filling: Combine cheeses in mixer or blender until smooth. Add remaining ingredients and mix well. Pour into chilled crust; bake at 350 degrees 30–35 minutes, or until a knife inserted in the center comes out clean. Remove from oven.

Prepare topping: Raise oven temperature to 475 degrees. Combine sugar, sour cream, and vanilla; spread over baked pie. Sprinkle crumbs over top and heat 5 minutes. Cool, then chill several hours before serving.

GREEK HONEY MOUNDS (MELOMAKAROUNA)

Yield: 96 cakes

$4\frac{7}{8}$ cups sifted flour
$\frac{1}{4}$ teaspoon salt
1 teaspoon baking powder
1 cup butter
1 cup shortening
1 cup honey
2 tablespoons orange juice
1 tablespoon vanilla
2 cups finely ground walnuts or pecans
$\frac{1}{2}$ cup confectioners' sugar
1 teaspoon cinnamon

Preheat oven to 350 degrees. Prepare Honey Syrup (next page). Sift together flour, salt, and baking powder. Melt together butter and shortening; transfer to a large mixing bowl. Gradually add honey while beating with an electric mixer. Add orange juice, vanilla, and half of the nuts. Continue beating about 15 minutes. Fold in dry ingredients a cup at a time. Knead until soft and pliable. Shape a teaspoon of dough into an egg shape and squeeze it nearly flat in palm with the fingers of the same hand. Bake on an ungreased baking sheet for 15 minutes or until light brown. In a small bowl, mix together remaining nuts, powdered sugar, and cinnamon. When cakes have cooled, dip in warm syrup and drain on a plate. Transfer to a clean plate and sprinkle with the nut mixture.

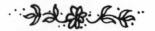

To liquefy crystallized honey, place the jar in a bowl of warm water (not warmer than the hand can bear) until all crystals melt. Honey will scorch if overheated. Granulated crystals will not harm the contents in any way.

HONEY SYRUP

Yield: 2 cups

1½ cups sugar
1½ cups water
2 tablespoons lemon juice
¾ cup honey

Heat sugar, water, and lemon juice to boiling, stirring until all sugar is dissolved. Boil 5 minutes. Remove from heat. Stir in honey. Cool.

QUICK PASTRY GLAZE

Yield: enough for 1 pie or 4 tarts

¼ cup honey
¼ teaspoon ground cinnamon
⅓ teaspoon ground nutmeg
hot baked pie or 4 tarts

Blend honey with cinnamon and nutmeg. Drizzle over top crust of pie or tarts, hot from the oven. With pastry brush, gently spread to cover crust. Delicious on apple, berry, cherry, mince, and peach pies. Before serving pumpkin or custard pie, drizzle Quick Pastry Glaze over each wedge.

Candies

HONEY FUDGE

2 cups honey
1 square unsweetened chocolate
$^1/_4$ teaspoon salt
$^3/_4$ cup evaporated milk
2 tablespoons butter
1 cup chopped nuts

Simmer honey, chocolate, salt, and milk for 5 minutes. Cook to soft-ball stage (240 degrees). Add butter; let stand until lukewarm; beat until creamy. Add nuts and pour into buttered pan. Cut when firm.

HONEY CREAM CHEESE FUDGE

1 package (3 ounces) cream cheese
$^1/_2$ cup honey
2 squares unsweetened chocolate, melted
$^1/_2$ teaspoon vanilla extract
$^1/_2$ teaspoon rum
$^1/_2$ teaspoon salt
2 cups evaporated milk
$^1/_2$ cup chopped nuts

Cream together cream cheese and honey. Add chocolate, vanilla, rum, and salt. Gradually add milk and nuts, mixing thoroughly. Spread in a buttered pan and allow to set for 2 hours at room temperature. Chill.

> *Homemade beeswax polish for furniture and floors can be made by shredding 1 pound of beeswax and a small cake of castile soap and dissolving it in water. Add 3 ounces of bicarbonate of potash. Heat gently in a large saucepan. Pour the mixture into a large basin and add 1 quart of turpentine, stirring continuously until almost cold. Mixture will become creamy.*

CHOCOLATE CLUSTERS

Yield: 24

1 package (6 ounces) semisweet chocolate pieces
3 tablespoons honey
water
$1^1/_3$ cups unsalted peanuts

Over very low heat or in the top of a double boiler over boiling water, melt together chocolate, honey, and water. Stir in peanuts. Cool 10 minutes; then drop by teaspoonfuls onto a cookie sheet covered with wax paper. Chill to harden. (Variations: Substitute coarsely broken walnuts and coconut or slightly broken pecans for the peanuts.)

The lifespan of a worker bee can extend to eight months or through the winter months, with the bee living in a semiconscious state through much of the colder months.

HONEY PENUCHE

Yield: 36–48

2 cups brown sugar
$^3/_4$ cup honey
$^1/_4$ teaspoon salt
1 cup milk
3 tablespoons butter

Combine sugar, honey, salt, and milk; cook over low heat to 240 degrees on a candy thermometer. Stir just enough to prevent sticking. Remove from heat, add butter, cool to lukewarm. Don't stir. When lukewarm, beat until thick; turn into a pan. Cut into squares when firm.

The word "honey" is derived from the Arabic han, becoming honig in German and hunig in Old English.

HONEY DRIED FRUIT CANDY

Yield: about 36 pieces

2 cups dried fruit (equal parts of any 2 or more fruits)
1 cup nuts
$^1/_4$ cup honey
$^1/_8$ teaspoon salt
1 cup dry flake cereal, crushed

Grind dry fruit. Chop nuts finely. Mix with honey and salt. Pack out in a flat sheet and flatten under a weight for 24 hours. Cut into desired shapes and dust with dry cereal. Grated orange or lemon rind may be ground in for variation.

LEMON BISQUE

Yield: 6 servings

1 package (3 ounces) lemon-flavored gelatin
$^1/_3$ cup honey
3 tablespoons lemon juice
$^1/_8$ teaspoon salt
$1^1/_4$ cups hot water
grated peel of 1 lemon
1 can (13 ounces) evaporated milk
$2^1/_2$ cups crumbs (graham cracker, vanilla wafer,
    or lemon wafer)

Combine gelatin, honey, lemon juice, salt, water, and lemon peel in a large bowl. Mix until well blended. Let stand. Mixture will turn syrupy in about 1 hour. Whip the evaporated milk and add to mixture. Fold in crumbs. Spread onto a baking sheet. Cool, then cut.

GREEK DATES

Yield: 36–48

$^1/_2$ cup honey
$^1/_2$ cup toasted almonds
$^1/_2$ cup chopped walnuts
$^1/_2$ cup diced orange peel
1 pound pitted whole dates

Mix honey, nuts, and orange peel. Stuff dates with mixture. To preserve freshness, wrap dates individually in plastic wrap.

Swarmed on a rotten stick the Bees I spy'd
Which erst I saw when Goody Dobson dy'd.

—John Gay, Pastorals

BUTTERED HONEY NUTS

Yield: 1¹/₃ cups

6 ounces unsalted nuts
1 tablespoon melted butter
1 tablespoon honey

Preheat oven to 300 degrees. Spread nuts on a baking sheet. Bake 15 minutes. Mix butter and honey and pour over nuts. Stir until nuts are completely coated with the honey mixture. Store in airtight container until ready to serve.

Protein with Honey
**Two tablespoons provide
the following amino acids:**

L-alanine	1,300 mg
L-arginine	1,200 mg
L-aspartic acid	900 mg
L-cysteine	10 mg
L-glutamic acid	1,500 mg
Glycine	3,500 mg
L-histidine	110 mg
L-hydroxyproline	1,000 mg
L-isoleucine	200 mg
L-hydroxylysine	150 mg
L-leucine	450mg
L-lysine	650mg
L-methionine	110mg
L-phenylalanine	350mg
L-proline	2,300mg
L-serine	1,000mg
L-threonine	300mg
L-tryptophan	65mg
L-tyrosine	100mg
L-valine	350mg

In early England, France, and Germany,
honey was considered so valuable that it
was often used in place of gold to pay taxes.

ALMOND CRISP

Yield: about ¹/₂ pound

³/₄ cup sliced almonds
¹/₃ cup honey
1 tablespoon butter or margarine
¹/₈ teaspoon salt
1 teaspoon vanilla extract
1 teaspoon grated orange peel
2 cups oat flakes

In a skillet, combine almonds with honey, butter, and salt. Cook, stirring constantly, over low heat until almonds are golden brown and mixture is thick and bubbly. Remove from heat and add vanilla, orange peel, and oat flakes, tossing until flakes are coated. Turn onto wax paper or well-buttered baking sheets, patting into a thin layer. Cool completely, then break into pieces. Best if you allow them to mellow at least one day.

Several queen eggs are laid to ensure the development
of at least one. The first to hatch will sting to death
any other young queens, often the first act of the new
monarch. To-the-death struggles ensue if two new
queens hatch at the same time.

HONEY PECAN BALLS

Yield: 36

>   1 cup butter
>   ¼ cup honey
>   2 cups sifted flour
>   ½ teaspoon salt
>   2 teaspoons vanilla extract
>   2 cups finely chopped pecans
>   confectioners' sugar

Preheat oven to 300 degrees; grease a large baking sheet. Cream butter; gradually add honey and beat well. Stir in flour, salt, and vanilla. Mix well. Add nuts. Form into very small balls and place on a greased baking sheet. Bake 40–45 minutes. Roll in confectioners' sugar while still hot. Cool on a wire rack. Roll again in confectioners' sugar.

> *The bee's tongue (glossa) is shaped like a bottle-washing brush. It is used to harvest nectar from flowers.*

PEANUT BUTTER–HONEY SNACKS

Yield: 24–36

>   1 cup honey
>   1 cup powdered milk
>   1 cup peanut butter

Blend ingredients thoroughly and form into small balls. Refrigerate until firm. Store, covered, in refrigerator. (Variations: Use chunky peanut butter; or add 1 teaspoon vanilla extract and chopped, roasted peanuts or soybeans. Roll in coconut.)

BANANA POPSICLES

Yield: 4

4 firm bananas
4 wooden sticks
$^1/_3$ cup mild-flavored honey
1 package (6 ounces) semisweet chocolate pieces
$^1/_2$ cup peanut butter
$^1/_4$ cup milk
$^1/_2$ cup finely chopped nuts

Peel bananas. Insert wooden sticks in fruit lengthwise. Chill 1 hour in refrigerator. In a saucepan, combine honey and chocolate pieces. Place over low heat and stir until chocolate pieces are melted. Add peanut butter. Continue cooking and stirring until mixture comes to a boil. Remove from heat; stir in milk. Dip chilled bananas in mixture to coat. Roll in nuts. Freeze. Serve frozen.

The stingless male bees—the drones—do no work.

CARAMEL CORN

Yield: 2–3 cups

$^1/_3$ cup honey
$^3/_4$ cup brown sugar
2 tablespoons butter or margarine
2–3 cups popped, salted popcorn

Combine honey, sugar, and butter in a saucepan; heat until sugar is melted and bubbling around the edges. Pour over popcorn and mix well.

*Democratic by nature, bees will vote on such decisions
as which place to live or which scout to follow
to the next nectar gathering.*

14

Health and Nutrition

The obvious benefit we realize from the honeybee is the food use of the product we know as honey. This "food of the gods" is widely recognized as both nutritious and delicious, but other beneficial aspects of honeybee by-products are less well known. There are many food and nonfood uses of honey, beeswax, and bee-sting venom.

The American Medical Association neither condones nor approves of most of the findings, reports, and opinions of bee-related medical studies made in this nation, but many physicians have suggested and prescribed honey or bee venom in treatments of many disorders. Medicinal salves with honey as a base are used for treating rheumatism, neuralgia, sciatica, and lumbago. Honey has been used in healing wounds and burns without infection because bacteria cannot live in honey. There have been successes in treatment of carcinoma of the vulva. Honey has been poured into "extensive" wounds and been helpful in their healing. Dr. Henrik Dold, a German physician, claims that the substance in honey responsible for bacteriological healings is an agent known as "inhibine." There are reports of doctors switching to honey as an antibiotic, using it exclusively instead of conventional antibiotics and antiseptics. These doctors claim that honey causes no ill effects such as most bactericides often do and also that honey is nonirritating, nontoxic, self-sterile, bactericidal, nutritive, cheap, easily obtained, easily applied, and effective. A doctor should be consulted in all medical circumstances where any doubt or speculation is involved.

Honey is easily assimilated into the system and does not exhibit addictive properties. Not only does honey not contribute to the many diseases linked to refined sugar, but it has also, in fact, been shown to be effective in treatments for intestinal ulcers and gastroduodenal ulcers. Eating honey regularly "immunizes" hay fever sufferers against spring pollen; chewing honeycomb offers immediate relief. Honey, glycerine, and lemon juice comprise an effective cough remedy. Fatigue can be overcome to some extent by eating an ounce of honey (around 300 calories) and inhaling deeply. The direct absorption of the honey (heat) with the intake of oxygen offsets the hydrogen ion concentration that causes muscle stiffness (contraction).

Honey can be used as a cure for hangovers or drunkenness because of its fructose content and catalase (an enzyme that speeds up alcohol metabolism) content. The presence of acetylcholine in honey, if taken in low concentrations, can lower blood pressure.

The presence of enzymes in manuka honey helps relieve indigestion. Honey is a readily acceptable and easily digested source of carbohydrates. Honey contains a variety of phytochemicals (as well as other substances such as organic acids, vitamins, and enzymes) that may serve as sources of dietary antioxidants. The amount and type of these antioxidant compounds depend largely upon the floral source or variety of honey. In general, darker honeys have been shown to be higher in antioxidant content than lighter honeys. There are over 300 floral sources for honey in the United States, including clover, alfalfa, buckwheat, and orange blossom.

Honey is classified by the U.S. Department of Agriculture into seven color categories: water white, extra white, white, extra light amber, light amber, amber, and dark amber.

STORING HONEY

At room temperature, crystallization begins within weeks or months (but rarely days). The crystallization process can be avoided with proper storage, with emphasis on proper storage temperature. For long-term storage, store honey in airtight, moisture-resistant stainless steel drums.

Different types of honey crystallize at different rates, and the specific mix of sugars and trace compounds in the honey influence how quickly it crystallizes.

Crystallized honey has not gone bad. You can liquefy it by placing the jar in a pan of hot water, but this will cause it to degrade, especially if you repeat the process.

Cool temperatures (below 50 degrees Fahrenheit) are ideal for preventing crystallization. Moderate temperatures (50–70 degrees) generally encourage crystallization. Warm temperatures (70–81 degrees) discourage crystallization but degrade honey. Very warm temperatures (over 81 degrees) prevent crystallization but encourage spoilage by fermentation as well as degrading honey.

TYPES OF HONEY

Most of us know honey as a sweet, golden liquid. However, honey can be found in a variety of forms.

Comb honey is honey in its original form; that is, honey inside of the honeycomb. The beeswax comb is edible!

Cut comb honey is liquid honey that has added chunks of the honeycomb in the jar. This is also known as a liquid-cut comb combination.

Free of visible crystals, liquid honey is extracted from the honeycomb by centrifugal force, gravity, or straining. Because liquid honey mixes easily into a variety of foods, it's especially convenient for cooking and baking. Most of the honey produced in the United States is sold in the liquid form.

Naturally crystallized honey is honey in which part of the glucose content has spontaneously crystallized. It is safe to eat.

While all honey will crystallize in time, whipped honey (also known as cremed honey) is brought to market in a crystallized state. The crystallization is controlled so that, at room temperature, the honey can be spread like butter or jelly. In many countries around the world, whipped honey is preferred to the liquid form, especially at breakfast.

Raw honey has not been heated or filtered. Filtration removes fine particles, pollen grains, and air bubbles and keeps honey liquid longer.

Honey is the only food consumed by humans that is produced by insects. Honey is an entirely natural product. It contains neither additives nor preservatives.

The number one killer in the United States—heart attack—may someday be tamed by honey-medicine research. Royal jelly or bee milk has been associated with controlling abnormal cholesterol and triglycerides in the blood.

Developments in bee venom therapy have shown positive results for all forms of rheumatic diseases and other degenerative disorders such as early cases of multiple sclerosis. The most widespread experiments and positive results have been reported outside the United States. Canadian and European researchers have for years successfully treated arthritis with bee therapy, yet the medical profession in the United States waves aside thousands of authenticated cures as old wives' tales. Records show that numerous cases of painful menstruation have been normalized by bee venom. Beekeepers as a group, exposed to stings in their apiary work, show relatively few signs of kidney trouble, bad eyesight, poor complexion, lameness, cancer, or paralysis.

The cosmetics industry has utilized the revitalizing and moisturizing qualities of honey in hand creams, lotions, and salves. Honey is a humectant, which means it attracts and retains moisture. This makes honey a natural fit in a variety of moisturizing products including cleansers, creams, shampoos, and conditioners.

Still another gift from the tiny honeybee is beeswax. With the highest melting point of all waxes—up to 140 degrees Fahrenheit—beeswax is used in candles, lubricants, salves, ointments, harness oils, phonograph records, sealing wax, furniture polish, varnishes, and comb foundations for apiarists.

Beyond the variety of food uses of honey that are exemplified in the recipes included here, there are many food and nonfood, practical and sensible benefits that we are just beginning to recognize and understand.

HONEY VS. SUGAR

The increasing use of sugar in the human diet has become a major concern of nutritionists worldwide. Many feel that we are in the throes of a nutritional crisis that may affect the evolution of the human race. Little is known about the effect of increased sugar consumption on human physiology since the trend is relatively new. The per capita intake of refined sugar in the United States is between 60 and 120 pounds per year. Americans consume approximately 1.3 pounds of honey per person annually. One startling fact is that the body has no physiological requirement for sugar; it furnishes only calories to the body, having no nutritional value. Refined white sugar has been proven to be both an addictive substance and a contributor to many diseases. Nutritionist and sugar expert Dr. John Yudkin says that a substance other than white sugar would have been banned by the Food and Drug Administration for demonstrating only a fraction of the negative effects of sugar.

Sugar is a carbohydrate, and carbohydrates are the major food supply and source of energy for the people of the world. Between 50 and 90 percent of human carbohydrate intake comes from grains, starchy vegetables, legumes, rice, wheat, corn, and potatoes. The remaining percentage basically consists of sucrose (cane and beet sugar), lactose (milk and milk products), glucose (fruits, honey, corn syrup), and fructose (fruits, honey). These sugars are different combinations of the same basic elements: carbon, hydrogen, and oxygen. The white stuff we know as table sugar is sucrose. It is a disaccharide—or multiple sugar—and requires digestive changes before assimilation.

Honey begins as sucrose and water in the form of nectar, but ends up only 1 percent sucrose after its conversion process. Honey is a pure, unprocessed food, consisting mainly of the sugars dextrose and levulose. It is 99 percent predigested, it is easily assimilated, and it is not addictive.

Honey does not contribute to the many diseases influenced by sugar. Childhood diseases proven to be caused, at least in part, by an excessive intake of refined sugar include rashes, infections, allergic manifestations, nervous upsets, malnutrition, vitamin deficiency, dental cavities, sugar diabetes, and addiction to sweets (often carrying over to alcohol addiction). In middle and old age, excessive sugar can cause arthritis, rheumatism, stomach and bowel gas, calcium deficiency (leading to tetany, heart diseases, muscular twitching, nervousness, tiredness, and bone diseases), certain allergies, obesity, vitamin deficiency, cancer growth, colds, sinus infection, tuberculosis, hardening of the arteries, high blood pressure and heart disease, coronary thrombosis, excessive blood sugar, duodenal ulcers, dental decay, gout, and dermatitis. Many of these problems are difficult to diagnose or to treat successfully.

Current research has shown that some complex carbohydrates raise blood glucose levels more significantly than certain simple sugars such as honey. Experts agree that people with diabetes can safely include a moderate amount of simple sugars in their diets.

Dextrose and levulose are the principal sugars in honey, but at least 12 more have been found in honey. Most of these minor sugars are not present in nectar (sucrose and water) but arise because of enzymic action during conversion or chemical action during storage. Honey has acids (negligible on a weight basis) that do affect the flavor and may be responsible in part for the excellent stability of honey against microorganisms.

One of the characteristics that set honey apart from all other sweetening agents is the presence of enzymes, complex protein materials that bring about chemical changes. Invertase, also known as sucrase or saccharase, splits sucrose into dextrose and levulose. Another enzyme, diastase, has been used as a measure of honey quality in several European countries.

Honey is not a suitable medium for bacteria for two reasons—it is fairly acidic and too high in sugar content for growth to occur. It seems to literally dry out the bacteria, a process known as the osmotic effect. In the resting spore form, however, some bacteria can survive, though not grow, in honey. Honey also contains vitamins (thiamine, riboflavin, ascorbic acid) and minerals (iron, copper, potassium, magnesium) not found in sugar.

When nectar is collected, it usually contains between 25 percent and 40 percent solids (mainly the disaccharide sucrose); the balance is water. The bee collects the nectar in a honey sac or "second stomach," which is a collection chamber functioning to receive and transport liquid foods. The worker returns to the hive to deliver the contents of the sac. As the nectar travels to the bee's proboscis, enzymes (principally invertase and glucose oxidase) act upon the solution in an "elaborating process." In a series of regurgitation actions, the droplets are exposed to the warm air in the hive (a constant 95 degrees Fahrenheit) and much of the nectar's water evaporates. The resulting substance, which thickens and is stored in open cells, later to be sealed, is honey, principally the monosaccharides dextrose and levulose.

Honey, then, does have advantages over sugar in its vitamin and mineral content and in providing flavor, but the main edge honey has over the white stuff is that it is a pure, natural, predigested food that is easily assimilated.

One tablespoon of honey, according to the National Honey Board, contains 64 calories. An equal amount of sugar contains 46 calories. Honey is also more expensive, but cooks tend to use less of it because it is considered to taste much sweeter than sugar. It is advisable to use recipes designed for honey, such as the honey recipes in this book, but honey can be substituted in most recipes calling for sugar. The general rule is to reduce the amount of liquid ¹⁄₄ cup for each cup of honey used. Honey may also be substituted for sugar, cup for cup. In baked goods, add ¹⁄₂ teaspoon of baking soda for every cup of honey used and reduce the oven temperature 25 degrees.

Since honey is believed to be sweeter than white sugar, many people use less honey per measure when substituting. On average, honey is 1 to 1¹⁄₂ times sweeter than sugar on a dry weight basis. My suggestion is to experiment with lesser amounts of honey in many of these recipes if you think they may be too sweet or if you feel that you should use less sugar in your diet.

Along with sugar, flour in the kitchen has come under close scrutiny and sharp criticism recently. Some nutritionists believe that unbleached flour has definite, if not obvious, advantages over bleached flour. Whole wheat flour is considered optimal by many cooks and, in fact, is found in many of the recipes in this book.

The main point here is that you choose what enters your mouth. Be smart about what you eat and still enjoy eating. Read about nutrition. Ask about it. Learn about it.

Here is a breakdown of honey's energy-boosting benefits:

Honey is a rich source of carbohydrates, providing 17 grams at just 64 calories per tablespoon.

Pure honey may be an effective form of carbohydrate to ingest just prior to exercise. When honey is eaten before a workout or athletic activity, it is released into the system at a steady rate throughout the event.

Honey is a great carbohydrate source to combine with post-workout protein supplements. Research has shown that ingesting a combination of carbohydrates and protein immediately following exercise (within 30 minutes) is ideal to refuel and decrease delayed-onset muscle soreness.

The crown jewel of all liqueurs—Drambuie— has honey as a base ingredient.

Honey, as a natural sweetener, does not result in heavy production of body fat as does refined sugar. When ordinary sugars (like cane or beet) are consumed, they must be broken down by digestive juices before they can be absorbed into the bloodstream and assimilated by tissue. With honey, little digestion is necessary, so absorption and the resulting energy boost occur quickly. Athletes of all ages can use honey as a nutritious and fast-working stimulant.

Simple cough remedy: warmed honey and lemon juice.

Honey applied to minor burns keeps air away from the skin, helps to lessen pain, and stops the formation of blisters.

An old Vermont concoction of apple cider vinegar (full strength, from whole apples) and honey—2 teaspoons each, with every meal— is claimed to be a general aid in treatment of most ailments: indigestion, insomnia, constipation, arthritis, ulcers, overweight, hemorrhoids, kidney trouble, and even excessive bleeding.

COLDS-GO-AWAY TONIC

Yield: 1 serving

2 tablespoons honey
1 tablespoon vinegar, light or dark
2 ounces brandy

Warm the honey and vinegar; add brandy. Take as needed. Rest and warmth are also suggested.

Beauty Treatments

DRY SKIN MOISTURIZER

Yield: 2 applications

> 2 tablespoons honey
> 2 tablespoons cocoa butter, melted
> 2 drops bergamot essential oil (optional)
> 1 drop lavender or tea tree essential oil (optional)

Mix all ingredients together and apply to clean, dry face. This all-natural moisturizer can be covered and kept in a cabinet, but it will solidify. For a second application, heat in microwave for 10 seconds, stir, and apply to skin as before.

FOAMING VANILLA HONEY BATH

Yield: 4 baths

> 1 cup sweet almond oil (light olive oil or sesame oil may be substituted)
> $\frac{1}{2}$ cup honey
> $\frac{1}{2}$ cup liquid soap
> 1 tablespoon vanilla extract

Measure the oil into a medium bowl, and then carefully stir in remaining ingredients until mixture is fully blended. Pour into a clean plastic bottle with a tight-fitting stopper or lid. Shake gently before using. Enough for four large luxurious baths. Swirl desired amount into the bathtub under running water—then step in and descend into a warm, silky escape.

HAIR CONDITIONER

Yield: 1 treatment

> $\frac{1}{2}$ cup honey
> $\frac{1}{4}$ cup olive oil (use 2 tablespoons for normal hair)

Mix honey and olive oil. Work a small amount at a time through hair until coated. Cover hair with shower cap; leave on 30 minutes. Remove shower cap; shampoo well and rinse. Dry as normal.

HONEY AND OAT EXFOLIANT

Yield: 1 treatment

> $\frac{1}{2}$ cup honey
> $\frac{1}{2}$ cup oats

Mix together and smooth over face. Massage and leave on for 10 minutes. Rinse off with warm water.

HONEY-KISSED LIP BALM

Yield: 1¹/₂ cups

1 cup sweet almond oil
¹/₂ cup beeswax
2 tablespoons honey

Place almond oil and beeswax in a microwave-safe bowl. Microwave on high for 1 minute or until mixture melts. Whisk honey into beeswax mixture; stir well. Set aside to cool completely. When cool, pour into small containers with lids. Apply to lips as a moisturizer or on top of lipstick for extra shine.

Honey and beeswax form the basis of many skin creams, lipsticks, and hand lotions.

MORNING BUZZ BODY SCRUB

Yield: 1–2 treatments

¹/₄ cup buttermilk
2 tablespoons honey
1 tablespoon grapeseed oil
1 egg white
¹/₄ cup freshly ground coffee
2 tablespoons wheat germ

In mixing bowl, combine buttermilk, honey, grapeseed oil, and egg white; mix thoroughly. Slowly add coffee and wheat germ, being careful not to clot or clump. Scrub should be smooth and creamy but with a slight grit. Allow to stand. Apply all over in shower or bath using a washcloth or body sponge to aid in exfoliation. Rinse completely. Towel dry and apply moisturizer. Chill remaining scrub if necessary. This scrub rids the skin of dry patches and aids in circulation. It helps to reduce cellulite while it firms and tones. Leaves skin smooth and supple.

PEPPERMINT HONEY FEET TREAT

Yield: 2 treatments

2 teaspoons fresh mint (optional)
4 teaspoons grated beeswax
4 tablespoons aloe vera gel
2 teaspoons honey
6 drops peppermint essential oil
2 drops arnica oil
2 drops camphor oil
2 drops eucalyptus oil

If using mint leaves, rinse and place on a paper towel to dry. Grind mint using a coffee grinder (or by hand using a mortar and pestle). Set aside. Melt beeswax using a small double boiler. In a microwave-safe glass bowl, combine aloe vera and honey, and mix well. Stir in beeswax. Let cool. Add mint and oils, stirring until completely mixed. Apply after bath or shower to entire feet and toes. Cover and store remaining mixture in cool place away from sun or heat. This treatment aids in circulation of overworked feet. It moisturizes and softens while it soothes and restores tired, aching feet.

PUMPKIN PIE ENZYME MASK

Yield: about 4 applications

3–4 tablespoons ground oats
1 tablespoon milk or heavy cream
2 tablespoons crushed pineapple
$3/4$ cup pumpkin puree, canned or fresh
$1/2$ cup honey

Mix ground oats and milk or cream in a bowl or mixer. Add crushed pineapple and pumpkin, draining excess water out of fresh pumpkin by squeezing it in a paper towel. Thoroughly blend the ingredients. While stirring, slowly drizzle in the honey, mixing well. Refrigerate in airtight container for 10–14 days. To use: Apply liberally with fingertips to face and neck area. Leave mask on for 8–10 minutes. Rinse with warm water and pat dry.

SIMPLY SWEET HONEY FACE SCRUB

Yield: 4 treatments

4 medium-sized strawberries
1 small cactus fruit
¼ cup oats
2 teaspoons green tea
3 teaspoons honey
3 teaspoons sugar

Wash strawberries and remove stems. Peel cactus fruit and discard skin. Slice in quarters; set aside. Using food processor or blender, combine oats, strawberries, cactus fruit, green tea, and honey. Mix until pureed. Place in glass or rubber mixing bowl. Stir in sugar until completely mixed. Apply small amount to cheeks, forehead, chin, and neck. Using fingertips and circular motions, work product into skin. Repeat. Apply more product as needed until entire face and neck are covered. May be left on skin for 10 minutes as mask or removed immediately. Rinse completely using tepid or cool water. Store remaining scrub in covered container in refrigerator for up to one week. This scrub exfoliates and softens while it moisturizes and brightens dull, dry skin.

To rejuvenate dry hands, a honey paste can be made by mixing together the white of an egg, 1 teaspoon of glycerine, 1 ounce of honey, and enough barley flour to make a paste.

SOOTHING HONEY BALANCING BALM

Yield: 2–3 treatments

- 2 tablespoons cocoa butter
- 1 teaspoon honey
- ½ teaspoon jojoba oil
- 1 drop bergamot essential oil
- 1 drop tea tree essential oil
- 1 drop lavender essential oil

In small double boiler, melt cocoa butter until clarified. Remove from heat and pour into small glass dish. Add honey and stir well. In a separate glass dish, combine essential oils with jojoba oil. Combine ingredients and stir well. Store in covered container in cool place away from sun or heat. Let stand until warm to the touch. Apply to face and neck and leave on skin or remove after 30 minutes using tepid or cool water. Balm protects skin from wind and cold and soothes dry, irritated skin.

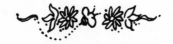

Index

Page numbers in italics indicate sidebars.